MW01040796

ISBN

Table of Contents

Welcoming you to the fiber-rich book of recipes.

Do you ever get fed up with having to eat leftovers for days on end because of all the recipes you make? Is that the case? If so, then this book is exactly what you need! Whether you're cooking for one or two, we've selected 150 simple, delicious, and quick recipes. That's exactly what I'm saying! All of the recipes in this book are designed to serve 2–4 people each, so they are quite economical.

No matter who you're cooking for, we've got you covered with everything from breakfasts to soups to entrees to desserts and beverages that are all appropriately portioned for two people (often with just enough for a second helping or leftovers for tomorrow's lunch!).

In college, I had a modest 2-quart slow cooker and spent a lot of time figuring out how to reduce recipes so that I didn't have leftovers for a week. I didn't have the freezer space to store more than a few days' worth of leftovers, so freezing was out of the question. There wasn't a neighbor I could drop off leftovers to because I hated throwing food out.

There are so many tales like mine out there! It has finally come to fruition thanks to all of you. We sincerely hope you and your partner enjoy these delectable dishes for two!

It's best to use a slow cooker

This Book Requires a Large Slow Cooker. What Size Do I Need?

All the recipes in this book are made for a slow cooker with a capacity of 112–3 quarts. Using a larger slow cooker will almost certainly not yield the results you desire. Cooking in a slow cooker requires that it be at least 2/3 to 3/4 full. Smaller batches will be required because these recipes are for two people. A slow cooker of the proper size is critical.

The Basics of Using a Slow Cooker

You'll need some time to get to know your slow cooker. Like your oven, each slow cooker has an own personality. (and your car). In addition, many contemporary slow cookers cook faster and hotter than their predecessors. With the increased focus on food safety, I believe that slow cooker makers have increased the temperature settings to make them more comparable to older versions. Consequently, these new slow cookers cook more quickly and at a higher temperature than their predecessors. In order to get the best results, you want to use a small, low-powered appliance like this. When we turn on the lights in the morning, we know we can count on it for the next ten hours or so. Never assume anything about your slow cooker unless you give it a try. You never know how temperamental it is or the temperature at which it cooks. Make the first dish in your new slow cooker on a day when you're at home to avoid disappointment. Several hours

the shortest time period stipulated in the recipe. Check to see if the meal is done before moving on to the next step. Alternatively, if you notice the aroma of cooked food, switch the stove off and save the meal.

Also, it appears that all slow cookers have a "hot spot," which is crucial to know if you plan to bake in your slow cooker. If you're not careful, you may end up with charred food in that region. Wrap some foil around the "hot zone" if you're baking in your slow cooker.

You Should Make A Note Of This...

In your cookbook, don't be scared to leave notes. It's all yours, so go get it! The chances are that your musings will be appreciated by a member of your family in the future. Make a note of the type of slow cooker you used and the time it took to cook the meal, so you don't forget. You won't have to think about it the next time. Apply what you've learnt to your next cooking endeavors. It's best to cook a recipe that calls for 7–9 hours of cooking in your slow cooker for 6–612 hours and then check the results. However, even if you overcook a dish, there is little you can do to fix the problem.

So, get to it!

Take everything out of the crock pot the night before so it can warm up to room temperature when you wake up. Then plug it in and turn it on as you're leaving the house.

If you're going to be gone for an extended period of time and need to prepare something that takes little time to prepare, do it the night before and store it in the refrigerator. When you go back home, reheat it. Alternately, prepare the recipes on the weekend when everyone is expected home and enjoy them during the week.

There are a lot of things you may not have known about slow cooking.

• As previously indicated, a slow cooker works best when it is about two-thirds to three-quarters of the way filled. It's possible that you'll need to increase or decrease the cooking time based on the amount of ingredients you've used.

• Do not place any of your vegetables on top of any other food. As a result, they'll be in closer proximity to the heat. The longer it takes your slow cooker to cook its contents, the fuller it is. Cooking time will be longer if food is packed tightly inside a pressure cooker. Finally, the longer it takes to prepare huge portions of vegetables, the more time it takes to cook them.

• It's time to keep the lid on the pot. You waste 20 minutes of cooking time for each glimpse. Every time you lift the lid, please keep this in mind! I understand that some of you can't help but lift. Adding 20 minutes of cooking time for each peek is always a good idea.

• In some cases, removing the lid is a good idea. If you want your dish to thicken, you can add more flour.

Towards the end of the cooking process, remove the lid a little bit.

You'll want to keep an eye on it! Don't forget to keep it away from youngsters, as well as your own safety!

Cooking Temperatures: 140–145°F (medium), and 160°F (well done) (well-done); 145–150°F for medium; 160°F for well-done (well-done) • 165°F for turkey and chicken

For maximum flavor, add fresh herbs 10 minutes before cooking is finished.

Before serving: • If your recipe calls for cooked pasta, add it to your dish 10 minutes before it's done cooking; 30 minutes before it's done cooking if the cooker is on Low. As a result, the spaghetti will not become soggy.

5 minutes prior to the conclusion of the cooking time, whisk in any sour cream or cream called for in the recipe. You don't want it to boil or simmer at all.

It's important to keep in mind that every slow cooker is a little bit different. • High—212°F–300°F

• Low—170°F–200°F

• Simmer—185°F

• Warm—165°F

Cooked beans can be frozen. First, remove the air from the freezer bags or boxes before storing them. Measurements for cooked and dry beans: In a 16-oz. can, drained, you get around 134 cups of beans It's around 2 cups for a can of 19-ounce beans, drained.

• 5 cups cooked beans from 1 pound of dried beans (about 2 12 cups).

Maple Breakfast Bake Hope Comerford, Clinton Township, MI

Prep. Time: 15 minutes

Cooking Time: 3–3½ hours

Ideal slow-cooker size: 2-qt.

3 eggs

½ cup gluten-free or regular baking mix ½ cup shredded Colby jack

1 cup milk

Cheese

¼ tsp. salt ⅛ tsp. pepper 6 maple flavored gluten-free or regular links, browned, chopped ¼ cup diced onion maple syrup, optional

1. Spray the crock with nonstick spray.

2. In a bowl, mix together the eggs, baking mix, shredded cheese, milk, salt, and pepper. Stir in the and onion. Spread this mixture out evenly over the bottom of the crock.

3. Cover and cook on Low for 3–3½ hours.

4. Serve with maple syrup drizzled over the top, if desired.

Divided into 2 portions, made with regular baking mix, before adding syrup, each portion contains:

Calories: 505   Fat: 38g   Sodium: 1655mg

Carbs: 49g   Sugar: 10g   Protein: 32g

- Gluten-Free
- Soy-Free
- Nut-Free

Bring-on-the-Bacon Brunch Hope Comerford, Clinton Township, MI

Prep. Time: 15 minutes

Cooking Time: 2–3 hours

Ideal slow-cooker size: 2- qt.

5 oz. Brussels sprouts, thinly sliced 4 slices bacon, cooked, chopped ¼ cup shredded Swiss cheese ½ cup sour cream ½ cup low-fat cottage cheese ¼ cup gluten-free or regular baking mix 2 Tbsp. butter, melted

1 egg

1. Spray crock with nonstick spray.

2. Spread the Brussels sprouts out evenly across the bottom of the crock. Sprinkle the bacon evenly across the top, followed by the Swiss cheese.

3. In a blender or food processor, blend together the sour cream, cottage cheese, baking mix, butter, and egg until smooth. Pour this mixture over the contents in the crock.

4. Cover and cook on Low for 2–3 hours.

Makes 2 servings. Each serving contains:

Calories: 510	Fat: 33g	Sodium: 733mg
Carbs: 20g	Sugar: 4g	Protein: 21g

- Gluten-Free
- Soy-Free
- Nut-Free

Breakfast-in-a-Crock Hope Comerford, Clinton Township, MI

Prep. Time: 15 minutes Cooking

Time: 3–4 hours

Ideal slow-cooker size: 2- qt.

1½ cups shredded gluten-free or regular frozen hash browns ½ cup diced cooked ham ¼ cup diced onion ½ cup shredded cheddar cheese

4 eggs

1 Tbsp. milk ¼ tsp. salt ¼ tsp. onion powder ¼ tsp. garlic powder dash of hot sauce

1. Spray crock with nonstick spray.

2. Spread the hash browns evenly across the bottom of the crock, followed by a layer of the ham, then the onion, then the cheese.

3. In a bowl, whisk together the eggs, milk, salt, onion powder, garlic powder, and dash of hot sauce. Pour this over the contents of the crock.

4. Cover and cook on Low for 3–4 hours.

Makes 2 servings. Each serving contains:

Calories: 467   Fat: 26g   Sodium: 723mg

Carbs: 26g   Sugar: 1g   Protein: 30g

- Gluten-Free
- Soy-Free
- Nut-Free

Ham and Swiss Breakfast Casserole Hope Comerford, Clinton Township, MI

Prep. Time: 15 minutes Cooking

Time: 3–4 hours

Ideal slow-cooker size: 2- qt.

5 slices gluten-free bread or 3–4 slices regular bread, crust trimmed off

1 cup shredded Swiss cheese

½ cup cooked ham, chopped ¼ cup chopped onion

3 eggs

½ cup unsweetened almond milk ½ tsp. salt ¼ tsp. dried dill ¼ tsp. dried parsley ⅛ tsp. pepper dash of hot sauce

1. Line the crock with parchment paper.

2. Press the bread into the bottom of the crock and up the sides about 1 inch to form a crust.

3. Sprinkle the Swiss cheese, ham, and onion evenly over the crust.

4. In a bowl, whisk together the eggs, almond milk, salt, dill, parsley, pepper, and hot sauce. Pour over the contents of the crock.

5. Cover and cook on Low for 3–4 hours, or until a knife comes out clean from the center.

Makes 2 servings. Using gluten-free bread, each serving contains:

Calories: 615   Fat: 30g   Sodium: 1228mg

Carbs: 36g   Sugar: 5g   Protein: 38g

- Gluten-Free
- Soy-Free
- Nut-Free

Southwest Breakfast Burritos MarJanita Geigley, Lancaster, PA

Prep. Time: 30 minutes Cooking

Time: 2 hours

Ideal slow-cooker size: 3-qt.

¼ lb. bulk , browned and drained

1 chopped green pepper

¼ cup chopped onion 1 Tbsp. melted butter

4 scrambled eggs

¼ tsp. salt ⅛ tsp. pepper ¼ tsp. chives ¼ tsp. cilantro

1 cup shredded cheddar cheese flour tortillas salsa

1. Mix all ingredients except flour tortillas and salsa.

2. Place mixture inside flour tortillas and roll up in burrito style.

3. Lay in a greased crock. Cook on Low for 2 hours.

4. Serve warm and topped with salsa.

Makes 2 servings. With 2 flour tortillas, cheese, and plain scrambled eggs, each serving contains:

Calories: 676   Fat: 48g   Sodium: 1083mg
Carbs: 21g   Sugar: 4g   Protein: 37g

- Nut-Free

Southwest Quiche Hope Comerford, Clinton Township, MI

Prep. Time: 15 minutes Cooking

Time: 3–4 hours

Ideal slow-cooker size: 3- qt.

1 gluten-free or regular roll-out pie crust (store-bought or homemade) ½ lb. bulk gluten-free chorizo , browned, drained ¼ cup diced onion

¼ cup diced red pepper 1 cup shredded Mexican blend cheese

5 eggs

½ cup milk

¼ cup salsa

¼ tsp. chili powder

1. Line the crock with parchment paper so it comes up the sides. Hanging over the top is okay.

2. Lay the pie crust in the parchment-lined crock and press it into the shape of the crock. You'll want to make sure the crust goes up about 2½ inches on the sides. You can crimp the edges if you wish.

3. Sprinkle the chorizo, onion, red pepper, and Mexican blend cheese evenly around the crust.

4. In a bowl, whisk together the eggs, milk, salsa, and chili powder. Pour this mixture into the crock.

5. Lay paper towel over the top of the crock and secure it with the lid. Cook on Low for 3–4 hours.

6. When the quiche is cooked, gently lift the parchment paper out of the crock, then slice and serve.

Makes 4 servings. Using regular pie crust, each serving contains:

Calories: 640   Fat: 49g   Sodium: 1438mg

Carbs: 22g   Sugar: 3g   Protein: 28g

- Gluten-Free
- Nut-Free

Broccoli Cheddar Quiche Hope Comerford, Clinton Township, MI

Prep. Time: 15 minutes

Cooking Time: 3–4 hours

Ideal slow-cooker size: 3- qt.

1 gluten-free or regular roll-out pie crust (store-bought or homemade) ½ cup chopped broccoli florets ¼ cup diced onion 1 cup shredded sharp cheddar cheese

5 eggs

¾ cups unsweetened almond milk 1 tsp. garlic powder 1 tsp. onion powder ½ tsp. no-salt seasoning blend ⅛ tsp. pepper

1. Line the crock with parchment paper, so it comes up the sides. Hanging over the top is okay.

2. Lay the pie crust in the parchment-lined crock and press it into the shape of the crock. You'll want to make sure the crust goes up about 2½ inches on the sides. You can crimp the edges if you wish.

3. Sprinkle the broccoli, onion, and cheddar evenly around the crust.

4. In a bowl, whisk together the eggs, almond milk, garlic powder, onion powder, no-salt seasoning blend, and pepper. Pour this mixture into the crock.

5. Lay paper towel over the top of the crock and secure it with the lid. Cook on Low for 3–4 hours.

6. When the quiche is cooked, gently lift the parchment paper out of the crock, then slice and serve.

Makes 4 servings. Using regular pie crust, each serving contains:

Calories: 390	Fat: 26g	Sodium: 399mg
Carbs: 21 g	Sugar: 1g	Protein: 14g

- Gluten-Free
- Soy-Free
- Vegetarian

Oatmeal Janie Steele, Moore, OK

Prep. Time: 15 minutes

Cooking Time: 6–8 hours

Ideal slow-cooker size: 2- qt.

2 cups milk

¼ cup brown sugar

1 tablespoon butter

1 cup dry gluten-free or regular oats 1 cup fruit (chopped apples, blueberries, cranberries) ¼ teaspoon salt

½ teaspoon cinnamon ½ cup fat-free half-and-half honey, optional (can be used for additional sweetness)

1. Spray inside of slow cooker with nonstick spray.

2. Combine all ingredients in a bowl except the half-and-half and honey, and mix.

3. Cover and cook 6–8 hours on Low.

4. Pour half-and-half in just before serving.

5. Add honey, if desired, to taste.

Makes 2 servings. Using ½ apples and ½ blueberries, each serving contains:

Calories: 560   Fat: 17g   Sodium: 523mg
Carbs: 85g   Sugar: 55g   Protein: 15g

- Gluten-Free
- Soy-Free
- Nut-Free
- Vegetarian

Oatmeal Cookie Oats Hope Comerford, Clinton Township, MI

Prep. Time: 5 minutes

Cooking Time: 7 hours

Ideal slow-cooker size: 1½-qt.

1 cup gluten-free or regular steel cut oats ¼ cup raisins

¼ cup turbinado sugar ¼ tsp. vanilla extract ¼ tsp. cinnamon ⅛ tsp. salt

4 cups vanilla almond milk

1. Spray crock with nonstick spray.

2. Combine all ingredients in crock.

3. Cover and cook on Low for 7 hours.

Makes 4 servings. Each serving contains:

Calories: 233   Fat: 7g   Sodium: 272mg

Carbs: 40g   Sugar: 34g   Protein: 6g

- Gluten-Free
- Dairy-Free
- Soy-Free
- Vegetarian
- Vegan

Coco Loco Oatmeal Hope Comerford, Clinton Township, MI

Prep. Time: 5 minutes

Cooking Time: 7 hours

Ideal slow-cooker size: 1½-qt.

1 cup gluten-free steel cut oats

¼ cup gluten-free or regular sweetened shredded coconut
2 Tbsp. coconut sugar ¼ tsp. vanilla extract ⅛ tsp. salt

4 cups coconut milk

1. Spray crock with nonstick spray.

2. Combine all ingredients in crock.

3. Cover and cook on Low for 7 hours.

Makes 4 servings. When made with full-fat coconut milk, each serving contains:

Calories: 663 Fat: 64g Sodium: 185mg Carbs: 28g Sugar: 22g Protein: 9g

- Gluten-Free • Dairy-Free
- Nut-Free • Soy-Free
- Vegetarian • Vegan

Cranberry Walnut Baked Oatmeal Hope Comerford, Clinton Township, MI

Prep. Time: 10 minutes

Cooking Time: 2½–3 hours

Ideal slow-cooker size: 1½-qt.

1½ cups gluten-free or regular old-fashioned oats ¼ cup turbinado sugar

¼ cup dried cranberries ¼ cup chopped walnuts ¾ tsp. baking powder ¼

1 egg

tsp. salt 3 oz. unsweetened almond milk

1. Spray the crock with nonstick spray.

2. In a bowl, mix together the old-fashioned oats, sugar, cranberries, walnuts, baking powder, and salt.

3. Add the egg and milk to the oatmeal mixture and combine well. Pour this into the crock.

4. Cover and cook on Low for 2½–3 hours.

Makes 4 servings. Each serving contains:

Calories: 248	Fat: 15g	Sodium: 348mg
Carbs: 30g	Sugar: 28g	Protein: 10g

- Gluten-Free
- Dairy-Free
- Soy-Free
- Vegetarian

Blueberry Vanilla Oatmeal Bake Hope Comerford, Clinton Township, MI

Prep. Time: 10 minutes

Cooking Time: 2–3 hours

Ideal slow-cooker size: 2- qt.

1½ cups gluten-free or regular old-fashioned oats ½ cup turbinado sugar 1 tsp. baking powder ½ tsp. vanilla extract ½ tsp. salt ½ cup

1 egg unsweetened vanilla almond milk ¼ cup coconut oil, melted ½ cup blueberries 1. Spray the crock with nonstick spray.

2. In a bowl, combine the old-fashioned oats, sugar, baking powder, vanilla, salt, unsweetened vanilla almond milk, egg, and coconut oil. Gently fold in the blueberries. Pour this mixture into the crock.

3. Cover and cook on Low for 2–3 hours.

Makes 4 servings. Each serving contains:

Calories: 281   Fat: 19g   Sodium: 475mg

Carbs: 23g   Sugar: 24g   Protein: 6g

- Gluten-Free
- Dairy-Free
- Soy-Free
- Nut-Free
- Vegetarian

Lemon Almond Blueberry Breakfast "Cakes"

Hope Comerford, Clinton Township, MI

Prep. Time: 25 minutes

Cooking Time: 3½–4 hours

Ideal slow-cooker size: 3-qt. oval

2 Tbsp. liquid egg whites ¼ cup coconut sugar 1 Tbsp. unsweetened applesauce ⅓ cup fresh lemon juice ½ tsp. lemon zest

2 cups almond flour ¾ tsp. baking powder ¼ tsp. baking soda ¼ tsp. salt ½ cup blueberries

1. Spray 3–4 small ramekins or individual baking dishes (about 1 each) with nonstick spray.

2. Mix together the egg whites, coconut sugar, applesauce, lemon juice, and lemon zest in a large bowl.

3. In a separate bowl, mix together the almond flour, baking powder, baking soda, and salt.

4. Slowly mix the dry ingredients into the wet ingredients. Stir only until just combined, then carefully fold in the blueberries. Pour the batter evenly into the ramekins or baking dishes.

5. Place a trivet, rack, mason jar lids, or crumpled-up foil in the bottom of the crock, then arrange the ramekins or baking dishes on top in the crock.

6. Place paper towel on top of the opening of the slow cooker. Secure it with the lid, then cook on Low for 3½–4 hours.

7. Eat with a spoon right out of the dish.

Makes 4 servings. Each serving contains:

Calories: 384   Fat: 28g   Sodium: 432mg

Carbs: 29g   Sugar: 11g   Protein: 23g

- Gluten-Free • Soy-Free
- Vegetarian

Baked Apple Delight Hope Comerford, Clinton Township, MI

Prep. Time: 25 minutes

Cooking Time: 4 hours

Ideal slow-cooker size: 1½– 2-qt.

2 large apples (of your choice) 1 Tbsp. coconut sugar or brown sugar ¼ tsp. cinnamon ⅛ tsp. nutmeg 1 Tbsp. finely chopped pecans ⅓ cup blueberries 1½ Tbsp. melted coconut oil Topping: 2 Tbsp. gluten-free or regular oats ½ tsp. coconut sugar ½ tsp. melted coconut oil ¼ tsp. cinnamon

1. Spray crock with nonstick spray.

2. Wash the apples. Cut the tops off, just enough to make them level and so the stems are removed. Scrape out the middle of the apples so that the cores are gone and some of the apple around it too. Leave at least ½ inch of apple around the sides. Be careful not to go through the bottom of the apple.

3. In a bowl, gently mix together the coconut sugar, cinnamon, nutmeg, pecans, blueberries, and coconut oil. Spoon this mixture evenly into the apples.

4. In a small bowl, mix the topping ingredients. Sprinkle this over the top of apples.

5. Place the apples in the crock. Cover and cook on Low for 4 hours.

Makes 2 servings. Each serving contains:

Calories: 320 Fat: 14g Sodium: 17mg Carbs: 49g Sugar: 34g Protein: 3 g

- Gluten-Free • Dairy-Free • Soy-Free
- Vegetarian • Vegan

Drunken Bites Hope Comerford, Clinton Township, MI

Prep. Time: 5 minutes

Cooking Time: 2 hours

Ideal slow-cooker size: 1½-qt.

3 sweet Italian links, cut into ½-inch pieces (gluten-free or regular) ½ cup merlot 1 Tbsp. red currant jelly ½ tsp. Worcestershire sauce (gluten-free or regular)

1. Spray crock with nonstick spray.

2. Place the Italian in the crock.

3. In a bowl, combine the merlot, red currant jelly, and Worcestershire sauce. Pour this over the s and stir them to coat all evenly.

4. Cover and cook on Low for 2 hours.

Makes 4 servings. Each serving contains:

Calories: 242	Fat: 16g	Sodium: 1160mg
Carbs: 7g	Sugar: 5g	Protein: 11g

- Gluten-Free
- Dairy-Free
- Nut-Free

Sweeties Hope Comerford, Clinton Township, MI

Prep. Time: 20 minutes

Cooking Time: 4–5 hours

Ideal slow-cooker size: 2- qt.

3 chicken links, cut into ½-inch diagonal pieces (gluten-free or regular) ¼ cup chopped red pepper 3 Tbsp. chopped onion 1 clove garlic, minced 3 Tbsp. chili sauce 3 Tbsp. apple jelly ½ tsp. gluten-free or regular soy sauce ¼ tsp. salt ¼ tsp. ginger ⅛ tsp. pepper ½ tsp. cornstarch ½ tsp. water

1. Place chicken , red pepper, and onion in crock.

2. In a small bowl, mix together the garlic, chili sauce, apple jelly, soy sauce, salt, ginger, and pepper. Pour this over the contents of the crock.

3. Cover and cook on Low for 3¾–4¾ hours.

4. Mix together the cornstarch and water, then stir it through the contents of the crock. Cook on High for an additional 15 minutes.

Makes 4 servings. Each serving contains:

Calories: 98   Fat: 2g   Sodium: 514mg

Carbs: 15g   Sugar: 13g   Protein: 4g

•   Gluten-Free •   Dairy-Free •   Nut-Free

Buffalo Chicken Dip (Hot and Spicy) Ne'cole Cichowlas, Chesterfield, MI

Prep. Time: 5 minutes

Cooking Time: 4 hours

Ideal slow-cooker size: 1½-qt.

2 oz. canned chicken (about ½ can), shredded well ¼ cup ranch dressing ¼ cup Frank's RedHot Original Cayenne Pepper Sauce 2 tablespoons Frank's RedHot Buffalo Wings Sauce 2 oz. cream cheese ½ cup shredded cheddar cheese celery sticks or tortilla chips for dipping

1. Place all ingredients in crock.

2. Cover and cook on High for 1 hour and then mix well.

3. Continue to cook on Low 2–3 hours.

4. Stir before serving.

Serving Suggestion: We love to eat this dip with tortilla chips, but experiment with your favorite snack. This dip saves well and I enjoy eating it cold the next day!

Makes 4 servings. Each serving contains:

Calories: 198	Fat: 13g	Sodium: 1030mg
Carbs: 2g	Sugar: 1g	Protein: 8g

- Nut-Free
- Gluten-Free

Spicy Cheese Dip Laura Elwood, Milford, MI

Prep. Time: 15 minutes

Cooking Time: 30 minutes

Ideal slow-cooker size: 2- qt.

8 oz. spicy bulk 5 oz. diced tomatoes and green chilies 4 oz. (½ pkg.) cream cheese

1. Brown the in a pan.

2. Add the cooked , tomatoes, and cream cheese to the slow cooker.

3. Cover and cook on Low, stirring every so often until the cheese is melted.

4. Once hot and everything is combined, serve with tortilla chips and raw veggies like cauliflower, broccoli, or zucchini.

Favorite memory of sharing this recipe:

The first time I had this dip, I was standing in a new friend's kitchen. We stayed up super late chatting about life and business. She gave me amazing business advice and made me feel so welcome on this new adventure I was on.

Makes 4 servings. Each serving contains:

Calories: 265	Fat: 23g	Sodium: 566mg
Carbs: 4g	Sugar: 3g	Protein: 11g

- Nut-Free

Chip Dip Janeen Troyer, Fairview, MI

Prep. Time: 20 minutes

Cooking Time: 1½–2 hours

Ideal slow-cooker size: 1½-qt.

¼ lb. bulk , browned 8 oz. Velveeta cheese, cut into chunks ¼ cup salsa

2 tablespoons milk

1. Place the and Velveeta into the crock. hot sauce, optional

2. Add the salsa and milk. You may need to add more milk if it is too thick. You can also add hot sauce to make it spicier.

3. Cover and cook on Low for 1½–2 hours. Stir frequently.

Serving Suggestion: Serve with tortilla chips.

Makes 4 servings. Each serving contains:

Calories: 240	Fat: 16g	Sodium: 1101mg
Carbs: 7.5g	Sugar: 5g	Protein: 8.5g

- Nut-Free

Cheesy Burger Dip Carol Eveleth, Cheyenne, WY

Prep. Time: 5 minutes

Cooking Time: 1½–3 hours

Ideal slow-cooker size: 1½-qt.

browned ¼ lb. Velveeta cheese, cubed 2 oz. mild taco sauce ¼ tsp. chili powder ¼ tsp. Worcestershire sauce ⅛ tsp. garlic salt

1. Place all ingredients in crock.

2. Cover and cook on Low for 1½–3 hours.

3. Stir once when cheese is melted. Eat with your favorite chips.

Favorite memory of sharing this recipe: If memory serves me correctly, my husband and I had this dip, chips, and a special drink on New Year's Eve while waiting for the year 2000 to come!

Makes 4 servings. Each serving contains:

Calories: 197   Fat: 11g   Sodium: 677mg

Carbs: 9g   Sugar: 5g   Protein: 12g

- Nut-Free
- Gluten-Free

Mexi Dip Hope Comerford, Clinton Township, MI

Prep. Time: 10 minutes

Cooking Time: 2 hours

Ideal slow-cooker size: 1½- qt.

4 oz. reduced-fat cream cheese ¼ cup nonfat plain Greek yogurt ½ cup shredded Parmesan cheese ½ cup salsa 1 tsp. gluten-free or regular taco seasoning tortilla chips

1. Combine cream cheese, Greek yogurt, Parmesan cheese, salsa, and taco seasoning in crock.

2. Cover and cook on Low for 2 hours.

3. Serve with tortilla chips.

Makes 4 servings. Each serving contains:

Calories: 127   Fat: 9g   Sodium: 777mg

Carbs: 5g   Sugar: 1.5 g   Protein: 10g

- Gluten-Free
- Soy-Free
- Nut-Free
- Vegetarian

Jalapeño Dip Hope Comerford, Clinton Township, MI

Prep. Time: 10 minutes

Cooking Time: 2–3 hours

Ideal slow-cooker size: 1½-qt.

½ cup vegetarian gluten-free or regular refried beans ½ cup salsa 2 Tbsp. reduced-fat cream cheese, softened ¼ cup chopped onion ¼ cup diced jarred jalapeños (hot or mild) ¼ tsp. chili powder ¼ tsp. garlic powder ¼ tsp. salt gluten-free or regular tortilla chips

1. Combine the refried beans, salsa, reduced-fat cream cheese, onion, jalapeños, chili powder, garlic powder, and salt in the crock.

2. Cover and cook on Low for 2–3 hours.

3. Serve with tortilla chips for dipping.

Makes 4 servings. Not including tortilla chips, each serving contains:

Calories: 35   Fat: < 1g   Sodium: 613mg

Carbs: 8g   Sugar: 1.5g   Protein: 2g

- Gluten-Free •   Soy-Free
- Nut-Free
- Vegetarian

Crab Dip Hope Comerford, Clinton Township, MI

Prep. Time: 5 minutes

Cooking Time: 2 hours

Ideal slow-cooker size: 1½-qt.

¼ cup nonfat plain Greek yogurt 4 oz. reduced-fat cream cheese, softened 2 Tbsp. fresh minced onion 1 clove garlic, minced ½ lb. gluten- free or regular imitation or lump crab gluten-free or regular crackers

1. Combine the Greek yogurt, cream cheese, minced onion, garlic, and crab in the crock.

2. Cover and cook on Low for 2 hours.

3. Serve with crackers for dipping.

Makes 4 servings. Not including crackers, each serving contains:

Calories: 135 Fat: 6g

Sodium: 430mg   Carbs: 6g   Sugar: 0.5g Protein: 11g

- Gluten-Free •   Soy-Free
- Nut-Free

Swiss Cheese Dip Ne'cole Cichowlas, Chesterfield, MI

Prep. Time: 5 minutes

Cooking Time: 3–4 hours

Ideal slow-cooker size: 1½- qt.

8 oz. finely shredded Swiss cheese ½ cup mayonnaise ½ medium sweet onion, finely chopped (almost shaved) Triscuits or your favorite cracker, for serving

1. Place cheese, mayonnaise, and onion in slow cooker.

2. Cover and cook on Low for 3–4 hours.

3. Stir well and serve with Triscuits or your favorite crackers.

Makes 4 servings. Without crackers, each serving contains:

Calories: 403 Fat: 23g

Sodium: 289mg   Carbs: 5g   Sugar: 1g Protein: 15.5g

- Nut-Free
- Vegetarian

Bacony Spinach & Artichoke Dip Hope Comerford, Clinton Township, MI

Prep. Time: 10 minutes

Cooking Time: 3 hours

Ideal slow-cooker size: 2-qt. 1 slice bacon, cooked, chopped 7 oz. jarred or canned artichoke hearts, drained, coarsely chopped 3 oz. fresh spinach, chopped 2 cloves garlic, minced 3 Tbsp. minced shallot ¼ cup mayonnaise 2 oz. reduced-fat cream cheese, softened ¼ cup shredded mozzarella cheese ½ tsp. salt ⅛ tsp. pepper gluten-free or regular crackers, for dipping

1. Spray crock with nonstick spray.

2. In a bowl, mix together all of the ingredients, then place them into the crock.

3. Cover and cook on Low for 3 hours.

4. Serve with crackers for dipping.

Makes 4 servings. Using canned artichokes, without crackers, each serving contains:

Calories: 178   Fat: 14.5g   Sodium: 655mg
Carbs: 5.5g   Sugar: 0g   Protein: 4.5g

•   Gluten-Free •   Nut-Free

Italian Veggie Spread Hope Comerford, Clinton Township, MI

Prep. Time: 20 minutes

Cooking Time: 5 hours

Ideal slow-cooker size: 2-qt.

¼ lb. Roma tomatoes, cut into ½-inch pieces 3 oz. eggplant, peeled, cut into ½-inch pieces 3 oz. zucchini, cut into ½-inch pieces 1 stalk celery, diced ¼ cup chopped sweet onion 2 Tbsp. freshly chopped parsley 3 Tbsp. pitted Kalamata olives, roughly chopped 1 tsp. capers 2 tsp. tomato paste 2 tsp. balsamic vinegar ¼ tsp. salt ⅛ tsp. pepper gluten- free crackers or pita crisps, or regular crackers or pita crisps

1. Spray crock with nonstick spray.

2. Place Roma tomatoes, eggplant, zucchini, celery, onion, parsley, Kalamata olives, capers, tomato paste, balsamic vinegar, salt, and pepper into crock.

3. Cover and cook on Low for 5 hours.

4. Serve hot, cold, or room temperature with the crackers or pita crisps.

Makes 4 servings. Without crackers, each serving contains:

Calories: 34   Fat: 2g   Sodium: 324mg

Carbs: 6g   Sugar: 3g   Protein: 1g

- Gluten-Free • Dairy-Free • Soy-Free
- Nut-Free
- Vegetarian • Vegan

Ranch Snack Mix Hope Comerford, Clinton Township, MI

Prep. Time: 15 minutes

Cooking Time: 2–2½ hours   Cooling Time: 30 minutesIdeal slow-cooker size: 2-qt.

1 cup Cheerios

½ cup gluten-free or regular rice square cereal ¼ cup unsalted cashews

2 Tbsp. sunflower seeds ¼ of a 1 oz. gluten-free or regular dry ranch salad dressing mix packet ½ Tbsp. olive oil

1. Spray crock with nonstick spray.

2. Place Cheerios, rice square cereal, cashews, and sunflower seeds into crock.

3. Sprinkle the dry ranch salad dressing mix all over the contents of the crock and drizzle with the olive oil. Toss gently.

4. Cover and cook on Low for 2–2½ hours, stirring every 30 minutes.

5. Spread mixture out onto a parchment lined baking sheet to cool for about 30 minutes. Store in an airtight container for up to 2 weeks.

Makes 4 servings. Each serving contains:

Calories: 128   Fat: 8g   Sodium: 201mg

Carbs: 17.5g   Sugar: 1g   Protein: 3g

•   Gluten-Free •   Vegetarian

Candied & Spiced Pecans Hope Comerford, Clinton Township, MI

Prep. Time: 10 minutes

Cooking Time: 3 hours cooling Time: 1 hour

Ideal slow-cooker size: 2-qt.

1½ cups pecans

½ egg white

½ tsp. vanilla extract 3 Tbsp. brown sugar ½ cup coconut sugar ½ tsp.

 Cinnamon ¼ tsp. chili powder 3 tsp. water

1. Spray crock with nonstick spray.

2. Place the pecans in the crock.

3. In a small bowl, whisk together the ½ egg white and vanilla until it is frothy. Pour this over the pecans and stir until they're evenly coated.

4. In a separate bowl, mix the brown sugar, coconut sugar, cinnamon, and chili powder. Pour this over the nuts and stir until they're evenly coated.

5. Cover and cook on Low for 3 hours, stirring every 20 minutes. When there are 20 minutes left of cooking, stir in the water and recover the crock.

6. When cooking time is over, spread the pecans out on a parchment paper– lined baking sheet. Let cool for 1 hour. Store in an airtight container for up to 2 weeks.

Calories: 280   Fat: 20g   Sodium: 49g

Carbs: 25g   Sugar: 17.5g   Protein: 3.5g

Makes 6 servings. Each serving contains:

- Gluten-Free • Soy-Free
- Vegetarian

Chicken Tortilla Soup Maria Shevlin, Sicklerville, NJ

Prep. Time: 30 minutes

Cooking Time: 6 hours

Ideal slow-cooker size: 3 qt.

2 stalks of celery, sliced down the center lengthwise, then chopped ½ medium onion, chopped ½ cup frozen corn ½ can black beans, drained and rinsed 3 cups chicken stock

1 cup water

16 oz. picante sauce 4 cloves garlic, minced ½ tsp. cumin 1 tsp. chili powder 1 tsp. paprika

1 cup diced precooked chicken

Optional toppings: green onion, chopped tortilla strips sour cream (or plain Greek yogurt) Mexican blend or taco shredded cheese jalapeños

1. Place the celery and onion in the crock.

2. Add the corn and black beans.

3. Mix well, then add the chicken stock, water, picante sauce, garlic, cumin, chili powder, and paprika.

4. Place the precooked chicken into the crock and mix well.

5. Cover and cook on Low for 6 hours.

6. Ladle into bowls and top with any or all of the optional toppings you want.

Makes 4 servings. Without toppings, each serving contains:

Calories: 163   Fat: 3g   Sodium: 831mg

Carbs: 20g   Sugar: 8.5g   Protein: 11g

- Nut-Free

Quilters Soup Janie Steele, Moore, OK

Prep. Time: 30 minutes

Cooking Time: 3–4 hours

Ideal slow-cooker size: 3- qt.

¾ cup diced cooked chicken 14½-oz. can chicken broth ½ of a 24-oz. jar Prego Roasted Garlic & Herb Italian sauce 1 Tbsp. parsley ¼ tsp. thyme

1½ cups cooked brown rice

1. Combine all ingredients in crock.

2. Cover and cook 3–4 hours on Low.

Makes 4 servings. Each serving contains:

| Calories: 190 | Fat: 4g | Sodium: 613mg |
| Carbs: 27g | Sugar: 7.5g | Protein: 11g |

- Dairy-Free
- Nut-Free

Black Bean Taco Soup Hope Comerford, Clinton Township, MI

Prep. Time: 10 minutes

Cooking Time: 5–6 hours

Ideal slow-cooker size: 3- qt.

14½-oz. can black beans, drained and rinsed ½ of 14½-oz. can diced tomatoes ¼ cup chopped onion ¼ cup diced green pepper ½ of a jalapeño pepper, seeded and diced 5 cups gluten-free or regular vegetable stock 1 Tbsp. gluten-free or regular taco seasoning

1. Combine all ingredients in the crock.

2. Cover and cook on Low for 5–6 hours.

Makes 4 servings. Prepared with vegetable broth, each serving contains:

Calories: 137 Fat: 1g

Sodium: 27mg   Carbs: 24g   Sugar: 3.5g

Protein: 7g

- Gluten-Free
- Dairy-Free
- Nut-Free
- Vegetarian
- Vegan

Cabbage Soup Hope Comerford, Clinton Township, MI

Prep. Time: 10 minutes

Cooking Time: 4–5 hours

Ideal slow-cooker size: 3- qt.

1 cup thinly sliced cabbage

14½-oz. can diced tomatoes ½ cup chopped onion ¼ cup diced celery ¼ cup diced carrots 1 clove garlic, minced ½ tsp. salt ½ tsp. oregano ½ tsp. basil ⅛ tsp. pepper 5 cups tomato juice

1. Combine all ingredients in crock.

2. Cover and cook on Low for 4–5 hours.

Makes 4 servings. Each serving contains:

Calories: 111   Fat: 0g   Sodium: 1163mg

Carbs: 22.5g   Sugar: 14g   Protein: 4g

- Gluten-Free
- Dairy-Free
- Soy-Free
- Nut-Free
- Vegetarian
- Vegan

No Fuss Chili Michele Ruvola, Vestal, NY

Prep. Time: 15 minutes

Cooking Time: 6–8 hours

Ideal slow-cooker size: 3- qt.

½ cup chopped onion 1 tsp. salt ½ tsp. pepper 15-oz. can tomato sauce 1½ tsp. cumin ⅛ tsp. garlic powder 1½ tsp. paprika 2½ tsp. chili powder 14½-oz. can red kidney beans water or broth to thin sauce, optional Optional serving ingredients:

Shredded cheese, scallions, sour cream, jalapeños, baked potatoes

1. Sauté ground in skillet until almost brown.

2. Add onion with salt and pepper.

3. Transfer to slow cooker.

4. Add tomato sauce, spices, and beans.

5. Add water or broth to thin sauce to desired consistency.

6. Cover and cook on Low 6–8 hours.

7. Serve in bowl or on top of baked potato with toppings of your choice.

Favorite memory of sharing this recipe:

When we go Christmas tree shopping we put this in the slow cooker and come home to wonderful smells in the house. As we decorate the tree we eat a warm, filling bowl of chili on baked potatoes.

Makes 4 servings. Without optional toppings, each serving contains:

Calories: 340   Fat: 12.5g   Sodium: 1436mg

Carbs: 29g Sugar: 6g Protein: 27g

- Gluten-Free
- Nut-Free

White Chili Janie Steele, Moore, OK

Prep. Time: 30 minutes

Cooking Time: 6–8 hours

Ideal slow-cooker size: 3- qt.

1 small onion, chopped 4-oz. can of chopped green chilies 2 cloves garlic, chopped, or 1 tsp. jarred minced garlic 1 tsp. cumin 2 15.8-oz. cans great northern beans, drained and rinsed 14½-oz. can chicken broth 1½ cups chopped cooked chicken shredded cheese, sour cream, and salsa for garnish

1. Combine all ingredients in slow cooker except cheese, sour cream, and salsa.

2. Cover and cook on Low for 6–8 hours.

3. Serve with shredded cheese, sour cream, and salsa for garnish.

Makes 4 servings. Without optional toppings, each serving contains:

Calories: 357 Fat: 5g   Sodium: 650mg

Carbs: 46g Sugar: 4g Protein: 30g

- Gluten-Free
- Nut-Free

Enchiladas Janie Steele, Moore, OK

Prep. Time: 30 minutes

Cooking Time: 4–6 hours

Ideal slow-cooker size: 2- qt.

½ lb. ground , browned and drained ¼ cup chopped onion ½ of a 10½-oz. can of cheddar cheese soup ½ of a 10½-oz. can of cream of mushroom soup ½ of a 10½-oz. can of Cambell's Golden Mushroom soup 5 oz. canned enchalilada sauce (mild or hot, depending on taste) ½ of a 4-oz. can chopped chilies

6 corn tortillas sour cream and salsa, optional

1. Combine all ingredients in crock except tortillas, sour cream, and salsa.

2. Cover and cook on Low for 4–6 hours.

3. One hour before serving, tear up tortillas and add to mixture.

4. Serve with sour cream and salsa, if desired.

Makes 3 servings. Without optional toppings, each serving contains:

Calories: 362   Fat: 16g   Sodium: 1568mg

Carbs: 38g   Sugar: 7g   Protein: 18.5g

• Nut-Free

Chili Burgers Carol Eveleth, Cheyenne, WY

Prep. Time: 10 minutes

Cooking Time: 2 hours

Ideal slow-cooker size: 1½- qt.

1 lb. ground 1½ cups cornflakes crushed to ½ cup ¼ cup ketchup 1 egg, slightly beaten 2 Tbsp. onion, finely chopped 2 tsp. Worcestershire sauce 1 tsp. chili 4 hamburger buns powder 1 tsp. seasoned salt

1. Combine ground , cornflakes, ketchup, egg, onion, Worcestershire sauce, chili powder, and seasoned salt.

2. Shape into 4 patties.

3. Broil or grill for 2 minutes or until seared on both sides.

4. Put in crock, cover, and cook for 2 hours on Low or until desired. Serve on toasted hamburger buns with topping of choice.

Makes 4 servings. Each serving contains:

Calories: 393   Fat: 15g   Sodium: 966mg

Carbs: 38g   Sugar: 9g   Protein: 26g

- Nut-Free

Cheesaroni Janeen Troyer, Fairview, MI

Prep. Time: 25 minutes

Cooking Time: 2 hours, plus 25 minutes

Ideal slow- cooker size: 2½-qt.

1 cup uncooked macaroni

½ lb. ground ½ of 10½-oz. can condensed tomato soup (do not dilute) ½ of 10½-oz. can condense mushroom soup (do not dilute) ½ green pepper, diced

1 cup grated chedder cheese ½ of 3-oz. can french-fried onions onion, basil, oregano, or Italian blend

1. Cook macaroni as directed. Drain.

2. In a large skillet brown with your favorite seasonings.

3. Add soups, green peppers, and macaroni and mix.

4. Place half the mixture in a greased crock. Sprinkle with half of the cheese. Top with remaining mixture and cheese.

5. Cover and cook on Low for 2 hours.

6. Top with the french-fried onions, re-cover, and cook for 25 minutes longer.

Makes 3 servings. Each serving contains:

Calories: 510	Fat: 30g	Sodium: 943mg
Carbs: 31g	Sugar: 7g	Protein: 26g

- Nut-Free

, Potatoes & Green Beans Ne'cole Cichowlas, Chesterfield, MI

Prep. Time: 5–10 minutes

Cooking Time: 2–5 hours

Ideal slow-cooker size: 2-qt.

6 oz. smoked , sliced into pieces on an angle 2 potatoes, cubed ¼ lb. fresh green beans 7 oz. low-sodium chicken broth ½ Tbsp. butter salt, pepper, and garlic, to taste

1. Place all ingredients in slow cooker, using the salt, pepper, and garlic to taste. Stir.

2. Cover and cook on Low 4–5 hours or High for 2–3 hours.

Favorite memory of sharing this recipe: This is one of our favorite meals; I have experimented with many different types of and loved them all. You really can't go wrong with this dish. It's a winner.

Makes 2 servings. Not including garlic, salt, and pepper, each serving contains:

Calories: 500 Fat: 32.5g Sodium: 1224mg Carbs: 31g Sugar: 2g Protein: 25.5g

- Nut-Free

Tramp Roast for Two Lori Stull, Rochester Hills, MI

Prep. Time: 15 minutes

Cooking Time: 4–6 hours

Ideal slow-cooker size: 3- qt.

1 cup sliced carrots

3 medium potatoes, quartered 1 onion, quartered ½ small cabbage, cut into chunks

4 cups chicken or vegetable broth

1-lb. pkg. Polish or kielbasa, cut in 3 inch pieces

1. Place vegetables in the slow cooker.

2. Pour broth over vegetables.

3. Place pieces on top of vegetables.

4. Cook for 4 hours on High, 6 hours on Low, or until vegetables are tender.

Favorite memory of sharing this recipe:

As a kid, my family would camp with a large group of people. We would always have a tramp roast together ... cooking giant pots of this over the charcoal grills. It was enough to feed an army, but I always loved it so much that I make small meals of it now. The flavors blend together so well!

Makes 2 servings. Each serving contains:

Calories: 611   Fat: 23g   Sodium: 3580mg

Carbs: 65.5g   Sugar: 25.5g   Protein: 53g

- Dairy-Free
- Nut-Free

Italian Bread Pudding Susan Kasting, Jenks, OK

Prep. Time: 20 minutes

Cooking Time: 2 hours

Ideal slow-cooker size: 3-qt.

1 lb. Italian , cooked and crumbled ½ onion, chopped

½ large loaf of Italian bread, cubed ½ tsp. oregano ½ tsp. basil ½ tsp. garlic powder

2 chopped tomatoes

1 cup shredded Italian cheese

¼ cup chopped parsley

4 eggs

1 cup milk

1. Mix together the , onion, bread, oregano, basil, garlic powder, tomatoes, and parsley in slow cooker.

2. In a bowl, mix together eggs and milk and pour over bread mixture. Let it soak in for a few minutes.

3. Cover and cook on High 2 hours. Top with cheese and cover and allow it to melt. Serve warm.

Serving Suggestion:

This is good with some marinara sauce on top.

Makes 4 servings. Each serving contains:

Calories: 686   Fat: 41g   Sodium: 992mg

Carbs: 39g   Sugar: 8.5g   Protein: 38.5g

- Nut-Free

Tacos for Two Michele Ruvola, Vestal, NY

Prep. Time: 10 minutes

Cooking Time: 5 hours

Ideal slow-cooker size: 2-qt.

2 chicken breasts

4 oz. zesty Italian dressing ¾ tsp. minced garlic ½ pkg. ranch dressing mix ¼ cup water

¼ tsp. chili powder ¼ tsp. ground cumin taco shells

Optional toppings: chopped jalapeños shredded cheese

sour cream salsa

1. Place everything but the shells and toppings in the slow cooker. Stir the ingredients a little to combine.

2. Cover and cook on Low for 5 hours.

3. Remove chicken from slow cooker when done and place on a cutting board. Shred the chicken.

4. Warm taco shells according to package directions.

5. Put chicken into taco shells, and top with favorite toppings.

Serving Suggestion:

Serve alongside a salad.

Makes 2 servings. Without taco shells and optional toppings, each serving contains:

Calories: 232	Fat: 1g	Sodium: 1163mg
Carbs: 4g	Sugar: 1g	Protein: 26g

- Nut-Free

Santa Fe Stuffed Peppers Maria Shevlin, Sicklerville, NJ

Prep. Time: 30 minutes

Cooking Time: 4–6 hours

Ideal slow-cooker size: 2– 3-qt.

½ lb. lean ground turkey or ground chicken salt, to taste

3Tbsp chopped onion

3 cloves of garlic, minced

¼ cup canned black beans, drained and rinsed 1–2 Tbsp. cilantro chopped pickled jalapeño, to taste ½ cup salsa

½ tsp. cumin ¼ cup frozen corn 2 whole red bell peppers, washed, cut in half, seeds and stems removed

⅓ cup reduced-sodium, fat-free chicken broth 5 Tbsp. shredded reduced fat Monterey Jack cheese, for garnish, optional

1 Tbsp. green onions, for garnish, optional

1. In a large skillet, brown the turkey and season with salt lightly.

2. When the turkey is browned, add the onion, garlic, black beans, cilantro, pickled jalapeño pepper, salsa, and cumin.

3. Mix well and simmer, covered, for 20 minutes.

4. Remove lid and add the corn and simmer until all the liquid reduces.

5. Drain if necessary.

6. Pack the peppers with the filling.

7. Place the bell peppers in slow cooker.

8. Add the chicken stock to the bottom.

9. Cover and cook on Low 4–6 hours .

10. During the last few moments, if desired, top with cheese and green onions.

Makes 2 servings. Without optional toppings, each serving contains:

Calories: 248   Fat: 7g   Sodium: 620mg

Carbs: 25.5g   Sugar: 10g   Protein: 19.5g

- Nut-Free

Vegetarian Stuffed Peppers Hope Comerford, Clinton Township, MI

Prep. Time: 15 minutes

Cooking Time: 5–6 hours

Ideal slow-cooker size: 3- qt.

1cup cooked brown rice

1 cup canned black beans, drained and rinsed ½ cup chopped yellow onion

¾ cup corn kernels

¾ cup chopped tomatoes 1½ cups shredded mozzarella, divided

1 Tbsp. freshly minced garlic ¾ tsp. salt ½ tsp. cumin ¼ tsp. chili powder 4 bell peppers (whatever color(s) you like), tops cut off and seeded ¾ cup marinara sauce

¼ cup water

1. Spray the crock with nonstick spray.

2. In a bowl, mix together the brown rice, black beans, onion, corn, tomatoes, 1 cup of the shredded mozzarella, garlic, salt, cumin, and chili powder. Spoon this into the 4 peppers.

3. Place the peppers into the crock.

4. In a small bowl, mix together the marinara sauce and water. Pour this evenly over the peppers in the crock.

5. Cover and cook on Low for 5–6 hours. 15 minutes before serving, sprinkle the remaining ½ cup shredded mozzarella cheese on top of each pepper and re- cover the crock.

Calories: 332	Fat: 10g	Sodium: 1064mg
Carbs: 48g	Sugar: 14.5g	Protein: 20.5g

Makes 4 servings. Each serving contains:

- Gluten-Free
- Soy-Free
- Nut-Free
- Vegetarian

South-of-the-Border Macaroni & Cheese Jennifer Freed, Rockingham, VA

Prep. Time: 20 minutes

Cooking Time: 2 hours

Ideal slow-cooker size: 2-qt.

2½ cups cooked rotini pasta 1 cup (4 oz.) cubed American cheese 6 oz. evaporated milk ½ cup shredded sharp cheddar cheese ½ of a 4-oz. can of diced green chilies, drained 1 tsp. chili powder 1 medium tomato, seeded and chopped 2½ green onions, sliced

1. Combine all ingredients except tomato and green onions in slow cooker; mix well. Cover; cook on High 2 hours, stirring twice.

2. Stir in tomato and green onions; continue cooking until hot.

Makes 2 servings. Each serving contains:

Calories: 279   Fat: 36.5g   Sodium: 1098mg
Carbs: 69.5g   Sugar: 15g   Protein: 37g

- Nut-Free
- Vegetarian

Spinach & Cheese Tortellini Ne'cole Cichowlas, Chesterfield, MI

Prep. Time: 5 minutes

Cooking Time: 5–6 hours

Ideal slow-cooker size: 3-qt.

6 oz. frozen cheese tortellini 2½ oz. fresh spinach 14½-oz. can Italian- style petite diced tomatoes

2 cups vegetable broth

4 oz. of cream cheese cut into chunks

1. Place all ingredients in slow cooker.

2. Cover and cook on Low 5–6 hours.

3. Remove lid. Give it all a big stir to mix well and serve.

Makes 2 servings. Each serving contains:

Calories: 535	Fat: 25.5g	Sodium: 897mg
Carbs: 57.5g	Sugar: 7g	Protein: 18.5g

- Nut-Free
- Vegetarian

Salmon Puff Jane Geigley, Lancaster, PA

Prep. Time: 10 minutes

Cooking Time: 2–3 hours

Ideal slow-cooker size: 3- qt.

½ of 1 lb. box of saltine crackers, broken 16-oz. can salmon 2½ Tbsp. butter cut into 1-inch squares 1½ cups milk

1. Place half of the broken crackers in the bottom of a greased slow cooker.

2. Pour the salmon over top.

3. Top with remaining crackers.

4. Place cut butter squares across the top.

5. Pour milk over the layers.

6. Cover and cook on High for 2–3 hours.

Makes 4 servings. Each serving contains:

Calories: 407	Fat: 18g	Sodium: 772mg
Carbs: 28.5g	Sugar: 5g	Protein: 30.5g

- Soy-Free
- Nut-Free

Atlanta Tuna Loaf Jane Geigley, Lancaster, PA

Prep. Time: 15 minutes

Cooking Time: 3 hours

Ideal slow-cooker size: 3-qt.

1cup flaked tuna

1½ cups bread crumbs

½ egg (beat egg and then divide in half) 1½ tsp. minced fresh parsley ½ tsp. salt ¼ cup chopped celery

½ small onion, chopped

⅛ tsp. pepper ½ of 10 ½-oz. can of cream of chicken soup

1. Mix all ingredients except the soup.

2. Shape into a loaf.

3. Place in a greased crock.

4. Pour soup over loaf.

5. Cover and cook on High for 3 hours.

Makes 3 servings. Each serving contains:

Calories: 382   Fat: 10g   Sodium: 949mg

Carbs: 43g   Sugar: 5g   Protein: 23g

- Nut-Free

Cheesy Broccoli & Cauliflower Hope Comerford, Clinton Township, MI

Prep. Time: 15 minutes

Cooking Time: 2½–3½ hours, plus 10 minutes

Ideal slow-cooker size: 2-qt.

2 eggs

1 Tbsp. cornstarch 1 cup shredded cheddar cheese, divided

¼ cup cottage cheese ¼ tsp. salt ¼ tsp. onion powder ¼ tsp. garlic powder ⅛ tsp. pepper ¾ cup chopped cauliflower florets ¾ cup chopped broccoli florets ¼ cup chopped onion

1. Spray crock with nonstick spray.

2. In a bowl, mix together the eggs, cornstarch, ¾ cup of the shredded cheddar cheese, cottage cheese, salt, onion powder, garlic powder, and pepper.

3. Stir the cauliflower, broccoli, and onion into the cheese mixture. Pour this into the crock.

4. Cover and cook on Low for 2½–3½ hours.

5. Sprinkle the remaining ¼ cup of shredded cheddar cheese over the top of the contents of the crock 10 minutes before serving and re-cover.

Makes 4 servings. Each serving contains:

Calories: 176   Fat: 12.5g   Sodium: 420mg

Carbs: 13g   Sugar: 6g   Protein: 1.5g

- Gluten-Free • Soy-Free • Nut-Free
- Vegetarian

Carrots for Two Hope Comerford, Clinton Township, MI

Prep. Time: 10 minutes

Cooking Time: 3–4 hours

Ideal slow-cooker size: 2- qt.

6 carrots, peeled, sliced into ½-inch thick rounds 3 Tbsp. water 1 tsp. coconut sugar 1 Tbsp. butter dash of salt

¼ cup fresh chopped parsley

1. Spray crock with nonstick spray.

2. Combine carrots, water, coconut sugar, butter, and salt in crock.

3. Cover and cook on Low for 3–4 hours.

4. Before serving, toss the carrots with the parsley.

Makes 2 servings. Each serving contains:

Calories: 135   Fat: 5.5g   Sodium: 172mg

Carbs: 25.5g   Sugar: 12g   Protein: 3g

- Gluten-Free • Soy-Free • Nut-Free
- Vegetarian

Orange Carrots Hope Comerford, Clinton Township, MI

Prep. Time: 5 minutes

Cooking Time: 3–4 hours

Ideal slow-cooker size: 1½- qt.

8–10 oz. baby carrots 2 Tbsp. orange juice 1 Tbsp. orange marmalade ⅛ tsp. salt

1. Spray crock with nonstick spray.

2. Combine all ingredients in crock.

3. Cover and cook on Low for 3–4 hours.

Makes 2 servings. Each serving contains:

Calories: 193   Fat: 0g   Sodium: 270mg

Carbs: 23g   Sugar: 16g   Protein: 2.5g

- Gluten-Free
- Dairy-Free
- Soy-Free
- Nut-Free
- Vegetarian
- Vegan

Summer Veggie Medley Hope Comerford, Clinton Township, MI

Prep. Time: 15 minutes

Cooking Time: 2½–3 hours

Ideal slow-cooker size: 2-qt.

½ cup chopped zucchini 1 cup fresh or frozen green beans, cut into ¾- inch pieces ½ cup chopped tomatoes ¼ cup diced onion 1 clove garlic, minced 2 Tbsp. olive oil ¼ cup water 1 tsp. butter 1 tsp. balsamic vinegar ¼ tsp. salt ¼ tsp. oregano ⅛ tsp. pepper

1. Spray crock with nonstick spray.

2. Combine all ingredients in crock.

3. Cover and cook on Low for 2½–3 hours.

Makes 2 servings. Each serving contains:

Calories: 123   Fat: 9g   Sodium: 26mg

Carbs: 8g   Sugar: 3.5g   Protein: 2g

- Gluten-Free
- Soy-Free
- Nut-Free
- Vegetarian

Barbecue-Worthy Green Beans Hope Comerford, Clinton Township, MI

Prep. Time: 15 minutes

Cooking Time: 3–4 hours

Ideal slow-cooker size: 2- qt.

½ lb. frozen or fresh green beans, cut into 1-inch pieces ¼ cup chopped onion ¼ cup ketchup 3 Tbsp. brown sugar 1 tsp. dry mustard ¼ tsp. salt

⅛ tsp. pepper 1–2 strips bacon, cooked, diced

1. Spray crock with nonstick spray.

2. Combine all ingredients in crock.

3. Cover and cook on Low for 3–4 hours.

Makes 2 servings. Each serving contains:

Calories: 173   Fat: 1.5g   Sodium: 422 mg

Carbs: 41g   Sugar: 34g   Protein: 4g

- Gluten-Free
- Nut-Free

Easy Greek Green Beans Hope Comerford, Clinton Township, MI

Prep. Time: 5 minutes

Cooking Time: 3–4 hours

Ideal slow-cooker size: 2-qt.

½ lb. frozen or fresh green beans cut into 1-inch pieces ⅓ cup gluten-free or regular Greek salad dressing ¼ cup diced tomatoes 2 Tbsp. diced onion 1 Tbsp. crumbled feta cheese 4 pitted Kalamata olives, chopped

1. Combine green beans, Greek salad dressing, tomatoes, and onion in crock.

2. Cover and cook on Low for 3–4 hours.

3. Stir in the crumbled feta and Kalamata olives before serving.

Makes 2 servings. Each serving contains:

Calories: 283   Fat: 10g   Sodium: 286mg

Carbs: 32g   Sugar: 20.5g   Protein: 13g

- Gluten-Free
- Nut-Free
- Vegetarian

Corn-on-the-Cob Hope Comerford, Clinton Township, MI

Prep. Time: 5 minutes

Cooking Time: 2–3 hours

Ideal slow-cooker size: 3-qt.

2 ears of corn (in the husk) ½ cup water

1. Place the ears of corn in the crock and pour in the water.

2. Cover and cook on Low for 2–3 hours.

Calories: 60   Fat: 0g   Sodium: 3mg

Carbs: 14g   Sugar: 2g   Protein: 2g

Each ear of corn contains:

- Gluten-Free
- Dairy-Free
- Soy-Free
- Nut-Free
- Vegetarian
- Vegan

Slow Cooker Baked Beans Anita Troyer, Fairview, MI

Prep. Time: 30 minutes

Cooking Time: 3 hours

Ideal slow-cooker size: 3-qt.

¼ cup diced onion 1 clove garlic, minced

6 slices bacon 16-oz. can Bush's Baked Beans 1 cup kidney beans, drained and rinsed

1 Tbsp. molasses ¼ tsp. chili powder 2 Tbsp. ketchup ¼ cup barbecue sauce 1 Tbsp. prepared mustard ¼ cup brown sugar

1. Onion, and garlic. Place into large mixing bowl.

2. Fry the bacon and drain. Crumble into the bowl.

3. Add the rest of the ingredients and mix well.

4. Put into a greased crock and cook on High for 3 hours.

Makes 4 servings. Each serving contains:

Calories: 448	Fat: 10g	Sodium: 1163mg
Carbs: 68g	Sugar: 41g	Protein: 15g

- Gluten-Free
- Nut-Free

Mexican-Style Pinto Beans Hope Comerford, Clinton Township, MI

Soaking Time: 12 hours

Prep. Time: 10 minutes Cooking Time: 5 hours

Ideal slow-cooker size: 3-qt.

6 oz. dry pinto beans water 1 tomato, diced 1 jalapeño, seeded, diced ¼ cup chopped onion 2 cloves garlic, minced 1½ slices bacon, cooked, diced ½ tsp. salt 5 oz. gluten-free or regular beer

1. Place pinto beans in a bowl or pot and add enough water to cover 2 inches over the beans. Soak at least 12 hours, then drain and rinse them.

2. Place the beans into the crock with all the remaining ingredients.

3. Cover and cook on Low for 5 hours.

Makes 4 servings. Each serving contains:

Calories: 186   Fat:1g   Sodium: 328mg

Carbs: 30.5g   Sugar: 3g   Protein: 10g

- Gluten-Free
- Dairy-Free
- Nut-Free

Healthy Barley and Lentil Pilaf Carrie Fritz, Meridian, ID

Prep. Time: 5 minutes

Cooking Time: 3–5 hours

Ideal slow-cooker size: 3-qt.

⅓ cup pearl barley ⅓ cup green lentils 1 Tbsp. butter 1 Tbsp. dried onion flakes ½ tsp. dried minced garlic 2 tsp. chicken bouillon

1 bay leaf

⅛ tsp. black pepper 1⅓ cup water

1. Add all ingredients to your slowcooker and stir.

2. Cook on Low 3–5 hours.

3. Stir and serve.

Favorite memory of sharing this recipe: This is one of my daughter's favorite dishes! She even likes to take the leftovers in her lunch box to school.

Makes 2 servings. Each serving contains:

Calories: 252   Fat: 6.5g   Sodium: 733 mg

Carbs: 39.5g   Sugar: 2g   Protein: 9g

- Nut-Free

Potato Cauliflower Mash Hope Comerford, Clinton Township, MI

Prep. Time: 10 minutes

Cooking Time: 6 hours, plus 10 minutes

Ideal slow- cooker size: 2-qt.

10 oz. Yukon Gold potatoes, cubed ¼ cup gluten-free or regular vegetable broth ¼ head cauliflower, chopped 1 Tbsp. milk 1 Tbsp. butter 1 Tbsp. sour cream ½ tsp. salt ½ tsp. dried dill ¼ tsp. garlic powder ¼

tsp. onion powder ⅛ tsp. pepper

1. Place potatoes and vegetable broth in crock.

2. Cover and cook on Low for 3 hours.

3. Add the cauliflower to the crock, cover, and continue cooking for an additional 3 hours.

4. At the end of cooking time, stir in the milk, butter, sour cream, salt, dill, garlic powder, onion powder, and pepper. Mash with a potato smasher or immersion blender.

5. Cover and let cook an additional 10 minutes, or until everything is heated through again.

Makes 2 servings. Each serving contains:

Calories: 249   Fat: 5.5g   Sodium: 667mg

Carbs: 41.5g   Sugar: 4g   Protein: 6g

- Gluten-Free
- Vegetarian
- Nut-Free

Sour Cream Potatoes Janeen Troyer, Fairview, MI

Prep. Time: 25 minutes

Cooking Time: 2 hours

Ideal slow-cooker size: 3-qt.

1 small onion

2 Tbsp. butter 1 lb. shredded potatoes 10-oz. can mushroom soup 1 cup shredded cheese

1 cup sour cream

1. Chop the onion and brown in the butter.

2. In a bowl, mix together the onion, butter, potatoes, soup, cheese, and sour cream.

3. Put in a greased crock.

4. Cover and cook on Low for 2 hours. Stir every 30 minutes while cooking.

Serving Suggestion: Goes well served with ham and green beans.

Makes 4 servings. Each serving contains:

Calories: 426	Fat: 30.5g	Sodium: 790mg
Carbs: 29g	Sugar: 5g	Protein: 19g

- Nut-Free
- Vegetarian

Luck o' the Irish Boats MarJanita Geigley, Lancaster, PA

Prep. Time: 30 minutes

Cooking Time: 4–5 hours

Ideal slow-cooker size: 2- qt.

2 large potatoes, washed and cut in half lengthwise 1 Tbsp. butter ½ tsp.

Salt ¼ tsp. pepper ¼ cup milk

browned and drained ½ small onion, chopped 3 bacon strips, cooked and crumbled ½ cup sour cream ¼ cup shredded cheese 3–4 rinsed clover leaves, for garnish

1. Place potatoes in slow cooker.

2. Cook for 2 hours on Low.

3. Scoop out pulp from the potatoes (leave ¼ inch in shells).

4. Mash pulp with remaining ingredients except cheese and clovers.

5. Spoon mixture into potatoes and allow to liberally top each potato.

6. Top each potato with cheese.

7. Cook potatoes for another 2–3 hours.

8. Garnish each potato half with a clover.

Makes 2 servings. Each serving contains:

Calories: 520	Fat: 38g	Sodium: 923mg
Carbs: 44g	Sugar: 3g	Protein: 32.5g

- Gluten-Free
- Nut-Free

Loaded "Baked" Potato Wedges Hope Comerford, Clinton Township, MI

Prep. Time: 20 minutes

Cooking Time: 7–8 hours

Ideal slow-cooker size: 3- qt.

1½ lbs. red potatoes, cut into wedges ½ cup shredded cheddar cheese 2 slices bacon, cooked, chopped ¼ cup chopped yellow onion ½ Tbsp. olive oil 1 tsp. salt ½ tsp. dried dill ½ tsp. onion powder ½ tsp. garlic powder ½ tsp. dried parsley ¼ tsp. pepper 1–2 Tbsp. chopped green onions, for garnish

1. Line the crock with aluminum foil, leaving enough at the top so that you can close it up into a packet with all the ingredients inside. Spray it with nonstick spray.

2. Place the potatoes, cheddar cheese, bacon, onion, olive oil, salt, dried dill, onion powder, garlic powder, dried parsley, and pepper into the foil packet you created. Stir to coat everything evenly, then close up the foil packet at the top.

3. Cover and cook on Low for 7–8 hours.

4. Serve with freshly chopped green onions on top.

Makes 4 servings. Each serving contains:

Calories: 418   Fat: 7g   Sodium: 712mg

Carbs: 31g   Sugar: 1.5g   Protein: 7g

- Gluten-Free
- Soy-Free
- Nut-Free

Cheesy Red Potatoes Karrie Molina, Freeland, MI

Prep. Time: 20 min.

Cooking Time: 4 hours

Ideal slow-cooker size: 2-qt.

1 lb. red potatoes, cut into small chunks or wedges ¼ cup chopped onion or ¼ tsp. onion salt ½ tsp. oregano salt and pepper, to taste 1 Tbsp. butter (cut into chunks) ¼ cup grated Parmesan cheese

1. Place potatoes in slow cooker.

2. Add onion, oregano, salt, pepper, and butter.

3. Cover and cook on High for 4 hours.

4. Sprinkle with cheese as you serve.

Favorite memory of sharing this recipe: My husband is a "potatoes" kind of guy and we always seem to have extra red potatoes for quick side dishes—so this is one of our favorites.

Makes 2 servings. Each serving contains:

Calories: 266   Fat: 7.5g   Sodium: 483mg
Carbs: 41g   Sugar: 2.5g   Protein: 8.5g

- Gluten-Free
- Soy-Free
- Nut-Free
- Vegetarian

Jack's Potato Pot Sue Smith, Saginaw, MI

Prep. Time: 20 mins.

Cooking Time: 6 hours

Ideal slow-cooker size: 2-qt.

½ of a 12oz. can evaporated milk ½ of a 10½-oz. can condensed cream of celery soup 3 strips bacon, fried and diced 12 oz. frozen hash browns

¼ onion, diced ¼ lb. Velveeta cheese, diced

1. Combine the milk, undiluted soup, bacon, hash browns, and onion in crock, then sprinkle the cheese over the top.

2. Cover and cook on Low for 6 hours.

Makes 3 servings. Each serving contains:

Calories: 344   Fat: 15g   Sodium: 1030mg

Carbs: 30g   Sugar: 10g   Protein: 13g

- Nut-Free
- Vegetarian

Sweety Sweet Potatoes Karrie Molina, Freeland, MI

Prep. Time: 20 minutes

Cooking Time: 4–7 hours

Ideal slow-cooker size: 2- qt.

1 lb. sweet potatoes, peeled, cut into pieces pinch of salt ¼ tsp. ground nutmeg ¾ tsp. cinnamon 2 Tbsp. dark brown sugar (packed firmly) ½ tsp. vanilla extract 1 Tbsp. butter

1. Place and mix potatoes, salt, nutmeg, cinnamon, and brown sugar in slow cooker.

2. Cover and cook on Low for 7 hours, or on High for 4 hours.

3. Add vanilla and butter.

4. Stir to blend or use hand blender to smooth.

Favorite memory of sharing this recipe: We love this recipe in the fall but is an excellent side dish year round. It helps with our sweet tooth as well.

Calories: 145   Fat: 3g   Sodium: 155mg

Carbs: 31g   Sugar: 13g   Protein: 2g

Makes 4 servings. Each serving contains:

- Gluten-Free
- Soy-Free
- Nut-Free
- Vegetarian

Happy Yams Hope Comerford, Clinton Township, MI

Prep. Time: 15 minutes

Cooking Time: 4 hours

Ideal slow-cooker size: 2-qt.

2 yams, peeled, chopped into bite-sized chunks 1 apple, peeled, cored, chopped 2 Tbsp. apple juice 1 tsp. lemon juice 2 Tbsp butter, melted ½ tsp. cinnamon

1. Spray crock with nonstick spray.

2. Combine all ingredients in crock.

3. Cover and cook on Low for 4 hours.

Makes 2 servings. Each serving contains:

Calories: 260	Fat: 11g	Sodium: 154mg
Carbs: 39g	Sugar: 10g	Protein: 2g

- Gluten-Free
- Soy-Free
- Nut-Free
- Vegetarian

Wild Rice with Cranberries Hope Comerford, Clinton Township, MI

Prep. Time: 5 minutes

Cooking Time: 3½–4 hours

Ideal slow-cooker size: 2- qt.

¾ cup uncooked wild rice ¼ cup diced onions ¼ cup dried cranberries ½ tsp. salt ⅛ tsp. pepper 7 oz. gluten-free or regular vegetable stock 1.

2. Cover and cook on Low for 3½–4 hours.

Combine all ingredients in crock.

Serving Suggestion: Sprinkle with walnuts (unless you want the recipe to be nut-free) and chopped fresh parsley.

Makes 2 servings. Each serving contains:

Calories: 338   Fat: 1.5g   Sodium: 377mg

Carbs: 72g   Sugar: 15g   Protein: 10g

- Gluten-Free
- Dairy-Free
- Nut-Free (optional)
- Vegetarian

Cheesy Rice Hope Comerford, Clinton Township, MI

Prep. Time: 5 minutes

Cooking Time: 3–4 hours, plus 10 minutes

Ideal slow- cooker size: 2-qt.

¾ cup uncooked brown rice 2 Tbsp. diced onion 1 Tbsp. butter ¼ tsp. salt ⅛ tsp. pepper 2¼ cups gluten-free or regular vegetable stock ¾ cup shredded cheddar cheese

1. Combine brown rice, diced onion, butter, salt, pepper, and stock in crock.

2. Cover and cook on Low for 3–4 hours.

3. Stir the cheese through the rice, cover, and cook an additional 10 minutes.

Makes 2 servings. Each serving contains:

Calories: 326	Fat: 21g	Sodium: 449mg
Carbs: 57g	Sugar: 0.5g	Protein: 16.5g

- Gluten-Free
- Nut-Free
- Vegetarian

Blueberry Torte Jane Geigley, Lancaster, PA

Prep. Time: 30 minutes

Cooking Time: 2–3 hours

Ideal slow-cooker size: 2- qt.

6 crushed graham crackers

2 Tbsp. butter, melted 3/8 cup sugar, divided

1 egg

4 oz. cream cheese, softened

½ can of blueberry pie filling

1. Mix graham crackers, butter, and half of sugar.

2. Press mixture into crock.

3. Mix cream cheese, rest of sugar, and egg until smooth.

4. Spread on top of graham crackers.

5. Pour blueberry filling over top.

6. Cover and cook on High for 2–3 hours.

Serving Suggestion: Serve warm with vanilla ice cream.

Makes 3 servings. Each serving contains

Calories: 395   Fat: 23.5g   Sodium: 337mg

Carbs: 71g   Sugar: 51g   Protein: 5g

- Soy-Free
- Nut-Free
- Vegetarian

Strawberry Cobbler Karrie Molina, Freeland, MI

Prep. Time: 10 min.

Cooking Time: 1½–4 hours

Ideal slow-cooker size: 2-qt.

½ of a 21-oz. can of strawberry pie filling (or cherry if you prefer) ½ of a box yellow cake mix 4 Tbsp. butter, melted

1. Place the pie filling at the bottom of the slow cooker.

2. Mix the cake and butter in a separate bowl.

3. Sprinkle over pie filling (do not mix).

4. Cover and cook on Low for 3–4 hours, or High for 1½–2 hours.

Serving Suggestion: You can place ice cream alongside or whipped topping on individual servings.

Favorite memory of sharing this recipe: My husband and I enjoy this because it reminds us of pie without all the extra effort. We have enjoyed it over vanilla ice cream and with whipped topping on top.

Makes 4 servings. Before adding topping, each serving contains:

Calories: 396   Fat: 15.5g   Sodium: 502mg

Carbs: 61.5g   Sugar: 40g   Protein: 1g

- Soy-Free
- Nut-Free
- Vegetarian

No-Sugar-Added Cherry Cobbler Janie Steele, Moore, OK

Prep. Time: 20 minutes

Cooking Time: 1–2 hours

Ideal slow-cooker size: 2- qt.

20-oz. can no-sugar-added cherry pie filling (can use other flavors)

1 cup flour

¼ cup melted butter ½ cup skim milk 1½ tsp. baking powder ½ tsp. almond extract ¼ tsp. salt ice cream or whipped topping, optional

1. Grease crock.

2. Combine all but optional ingredients, reserving a little of the cherry pie filling to pour over the top just before serving the cobbler. Mix until smooth.

3. Cover and cook for 1–2 hours, or until heated through.

4. Serve with ice cream or whipped topping, if desired.

Makes 4 servings. Before adding topping, each serving contains:

Calories: 279   Fat: 11g   Sodium: 442mg

Carbs: 25g   Sugar: 8g   Protein: 5g

- Soy-Free
- Vegetarian

Munchy Rhubarby Crunch Jane Geigley, Lancaster, PA

Prep. Time: 30 minutes

Cooking Time: 2–3 hours

Ideal slow-cooker size: 2- qt.

½ cup sifted flour 3/8 cup uncooked oatmeal ½ cup brown sugar 4 Tbsp. butter, melted ½ tsp. cinnamon

2cups diced rhubarb

½ cup sugar 1 Tbsp. cornstarch ½ cup water

½ tsp. vanilla extract

1. Mix flour, oatmeal, brown sugar, butter, and cinnamon to make crumbs.

2. Press half of the crumbs into greased crock.

3. Layer rhubarb over top.

4. Mix sugar, cornstarch, water, and vanilla in small pan and cook until thick and clear (constantly stirring).

5. Pour over rhubarb.

6. Top with remaining crumbs.

7. Cover and cook on High for 2–3 hours.

Makes 3 servings. Each serving contains:

Calories: 515   Fat: 15g   Sodium: 112mg

Carbs: 114g   Sugar: 86g   Protein: 4.5g

- Soy-Free
- Nut-Free
- Vegetarian

Amazing Caramel Apple Crunch Hope Comerford, Clinton Township, MI

Prep. Time: 20 minutes

Cooking Time: 4 hours Cooling Time: 1 hour

Ideal slow-cooker size: 2-qt.

½ cup brown sugar ¼ cup turbinado sugar 2–3 Honeycrisp apples, cut into bite-sized chunks ½ tsp. cinnamon ½ tsp. vanilla extract ½ tsp. cornstarch dash of nutmeg ⅛ tsp. salt Crumble: ⅓ cup gluten-free or regular old-fashioned oats ⅓ cup brown sugar 2 Tbsp. almond flour ¼ tsp. cinnamon 1½ Tbsp. coconut oil, in solid but softened form, or butter

1. Spray crock with nonstick spray.

2. Mix the brown sugar and turbinado sugar together and spread it across the bottom of the crock.

3. Toss the apples with the cinnamon, vanilla, cornstarch, nutmeg, and salt. Pour evenly over the sugar mix at the bottom of the crock.

4. Mix the crumble ingredients together in a bowl with your fingers. Sprinkle this over the apples.

5. Cover and cook on Low for 4 hours. Let sit to cool for 1 more hour, with the cover off, before serving. This will allow the caramel to thicken.

Serving Suggestion: Serve over your favorite vanilla ice cream, or delicious vanilla Greek yogurt.

Makes 4 servings. Without toppings, each serving contains:

Calories: 333   Fat: 7g   Sodium: 73mg

Carbs: 83.5g   Sugar: 74g   Protein: 2g

- Gluten-Free
- Dairy-Free
- Soy-Free
- Vegetarian
- Vegan

Chocolate Cherry Cheesecake Crumble Sue Hamilton, Benson, AZ

Prep. Time: 10 minutes

Cooking Time: 1½ hours

Ideal slow-cooker size: 2- qt.

15-oz. can of dark sweet cherries with juice 3.4-oz. box of cheesecake instant pudding mix 12 double-stuff chocolate sandwich cookies, broken (I just use my hands) 4 Tbsp. butter, melted

1. Spray the crock with nonstick spray.

2. Pour the cherries in the crock. Add 4 tablespoons of the instant pudding and stir it in.

3. In a bowl, combine the broken cookies and the butter. Stir until well mixed.

4. Add the rest of the dry pudding mix to the cookie mixture. Spoon the mixture evenly on top of the fruit.

5. Cover and cook on High for 1½ hours.

Serving Suggestion: Serve warm with whipped cream.

Makes 4 servings. Before adding whipped cream, each serving contains:

Calories: 506   Fat: 21.5g   Sodium: 635mg

Carbs: 76g   Sugar: 61.5g   Protein: 1g

- Soy-Free
- Nut-Free
- Vegetarian

Apple Caramel Oatmeal Cream Betty Sue Hamilton, Benson, AZ

Prep. Time: 10 minutes

Cooking Time: 1½ hours

Ideal slow-cooker size: 2- qt.

3cups peeled and sliced apples

3.4-oz. box caramel instant pudding mix 4 oatmeal cream pie soft sandwich cookies, broken 4 Tbsp. butter 1 egg, beaten, or 4 Tbsp. egg substitute

1. Spray the crock with nonstick spray.

2. Combine the apples with 4 tablespoons of the instant pudding and stir it in.

3. In a bowl, combine the broken cookies and the butter. Stir until well mixed.

4. Add the rest of the dry pudding mix to the cookie mixture. Mix well.

5. Add the egg, stirring until well blended. Spoon the mixture evenly on top of the fruit.

6. Cover and cook on High for 1½ hours.

Serving Suggestion: Serve warm with whipped cream.

Makes 4 servings. Without whipped cream, each serving contains:

Calories: 392	Fat: 17.5g	Sodium: 535mg
Carbs: 56.5g	Sugar: 43.5g	Protein: 3.5g

- Nut-Free
- Vegetarian

Peach Pecan Delight Sue Hamilton, Benson, AZ

Prep. Time: 10 minutes

Cooking Time: 1½ hours

Ideal slow-cooker size: 2- qt.

15-oz. can sliced peaches with the juice 3.4-oz. box instant vanilla pudding mix, divided 12 pecan shortbread cookies, broken (I just use my hands to do this) 4 Tbsp. butter, melted

1. Spray the crock with nonstick spray.

2. Pour the peaches into the crock. Add 4 tablespoons of the instant pudding and stir it in.

3. In a bowl, combine the broken cookies and the butter. Stir until well mixed.

4. Add the rest of the dry pudding mix to the cookie mixture. Spoon the mixture evenly on top of the fruit.

5. Cover and cook on High for 1½ hours.

Serving Suggestion: Serve warm with whipped cream.

Makes 4 servings. Without whipped cream, each serving contains:

Calories: 501   Fat: 26g   Sodium: 697mg

Carbs: 62g   Sugar: 45g   Protein: 4g

• Vegetarian

Amish Shoo-Fly Melt MarJanita Geigley, Lancaster, PA

Prep. Time: 30 minutes

Cooking Time: 2–3 hours

Ideal slow-cooker size: 2- qt.

½ baked 9-inch pie shell broken into crumbles ½ cup flour

3/8 cup brown sugar 2¼ tsp. shortening ½ tsp. baking soda ½ cup boiling water ½ cup molasses ½ beaten egg

1. Place pie crumbles in bottom of greased crock.

2. Mix flour, sugar, and shortening until crumbly.

3. Set ¼ cup of the mixture aside.

4. Dissolve the baking soda in the water.

5. Add the crumbs to molasses, egg, and baking soda mix, keeping the 1/4 cup aside.

6. Place in crock.

7. Sprinkle the reserved crumbs over top.

8. Cook on high for 2–3 hours.

Makes 3 servings. Each serving contains:

Calories: 471	Fat: 10g	Sodium: 361mg
Carbs: 100g	Sugar: 69g	Protein: 4.5g

- Nut-Free
- Vegetarian

Peanut Butter and White Chocolate Andrea Maher, Dunedin, FL

Prep. Time: 10 minutes

Cooking Time: 3 hours

Ideal slow-cooker size: 3–4- qt.

¼ cup coconut oil ¼ cup coconut sugar ⅓ cup powdered peanut butter 3 Tbsp. gluten-free or regular oat flour 2 large eggs, beaten ½ tsp. vanilla extract sea salt, to taste 2 Tbsp. white chocolate chips 2 Tbsp. cup crushed macadamia nuts 2 tsp. white chocolate chips for topping,

Optional

2 tsp. crushed macadamia nuts for topping, optional

1. Line the crock with a large piece of foil; spray with nonstick spray.

2. Whisk all ingredients together except the chips and nuts for topping.

3. Place a piece of paper towel over the top of the slow cooker and secure with the lid. Cook on Low for 3 hours; the cake should be set around the edges and gooey in the center.

4. Serve warm in a pretty bowl. Sprinkle 1 Tbsp. white chocolate chips and 1 Tbsp. crushed macadamia nuts on top, if desired.

Makes 3 servings. Without optional toppings, each serving contains:

Calories: 386   Fat: 29g   Sodium: 359mg

Carbs: 30.5g   Sugar: 19g   Protein: 10g

- Gluten-Free
- Vegetarian

Gooey Chocolate Cake For Two Andrea Maher, Dunedin, FL

Prep. Time: 10 minutes

Cooking Time: 3 hours

Ideal slow-cooker size: 3–5- qt.

½ cup unsweetened applesauce ½ cup coconut sugar ⅔ cup unsweetened cocoa ⅓ cup gluten-free or regular oat flour 3 large eggs, beaten 1 tsp. vanilla extract sea salt, to taste ½ cup chocolate chips 2 Tbsp. peanut butter, melted, optional

1. Line the crock with a large piece of foil, spray with nonstick spray.

2. Whisk all ingredients together except the melted peanut butter.

3. Place a piece of paper towel across the top of the slow cooker, secure with the lid, and cook on Low for 3 hours; the cake should be set around the edges and gooey in the center.

4. Serve warm and in a pretty bowl. Drizzle some melted peanut butter on top if you desire.

Makes 2 servings. Without peanut butter, each serving contains:

Calories: 609   Fat: 21.5g   Sodium: 822mg

Carbs: 110.5g   Sugar: 63.5g   Protein: 20.5g

- Gluten-Free
- Nut-Free
- Vegetarian

Chocolate Obsession in a Slow Cooker Sue Smith, Saginaw, MI

Prep. Time: 15 minutes

Cooking Time: 2 hours

Ideal slow-cooker size: 3-qt.

1¾ cups light brown sugar, divided

1cup flour

¼ cup plus 3 Tbsp. cocoa powder, divided

2 tsp. baking powder ¼ tsp. salt ½ cup milk 2 Tbsp. butter, melted ½ tsp. vanilla extract ¼ tsp. almond extract 1¾ cup hot water vanilla ice cream

1. Stir together 1 cup brown sugar, flour, 3 Tbsp. cocoa powder, baking powder, and salt.

2. Whisk in the milk, butter, vanilla extract, and almond extract.

3. Spread into the slow cooker.

4. Mix the rest of the brown sugar and cocoa.

5. Sprinkle over the batter.

6. Pour in the hot water, but do not stir.

7. Cover and cook for 2 hours on High.

8. Test with a toothpick in the center; it should come out clean.

9. Spoon into dishes and serve with ice cream.

Makes 4 servings. Without ice cream, each serving contains:

Calories: 517   Fat: 8g   Sodium: 444mg

Carbs: 143g   Sugar: 114g   Protein: 7.5g

- Soy-Free
- Vegetarian

White Chocolate Coconut Dream Bar Andrea Maher, Dunedin, FL

Prep. Time: 15 minutes

Cooking Time: 3 hours

Ideal slow-cooker size: 3–5- qt.

2 large eggs, separated ¼ cup coconut sugar ½ tsp. vanilla extract ¼ cup melted coconut oil ½ cup organic unsweetened gluten-free or regular shredded coconut ½ cup gluten-free or regular oats

1 cup full-fat organic coconut milk

2 Tbsp. white chocolate chips

1. Spray your crock with nonstick spray.

2. Beat the egg whites with a hand mixer on high for 2–3 minutes until stiff peaks form.

3. In a separate bowl, beat the yolks with the sugar. Add the vanilla extract, coconut oil, coconut, and oats until thoroughly combined.

4. Slowly add the coconut milk. Gently fold in the egg whites until combined.

5. Pour the mixture into your crock.

6. Place paper towels over the top of the slow cooker opening and secure with the lid.

7. Cook on Low for 2–3 hours.

8. Top with the white chocolate chips and add a little extra shredded coconut, if desired.

Calories: 451   Fat: 37.5g   Sodium: 82mg

Carbs: 27g   Sugar: 15.5g   Protein: 7g

Makes 4 servings. Each serving contains:

- Gluten-Free
- Nut-Free
- Vegetarian

Orange and Peppermint Fudge Hope Comerford, Clinton Township, MI

Prep. Time: 5 minutes

Cooking Time: 2 hours Cooling Time: 4 hours

Ideal slow-cooker size: 2-qt.

¾ cups semisweet chocolate chips 3.5 oz. (¼ of 14 oz. can) sweetened condensed milk ¼ tsp. vanilla extract 1 drop orange essential oil (be sure it's food-grade) or ¼ tsp. orange extract 1 drop peppermint essential oil (be sure it's food-grade) or ¼ tsp. peppermint extract

1. Spray your crock with nonstick spray.

2. Place the chocolate chips, sweetened condensed milk, and vanilla into the crock.

3. Cover and cook on Low for about 2 hours, stirring every 30 minutes.

4. Line a 4x4-inch brownie pan with parchment paper, or spray with nonstick spray.

5. When the chocolate is completely liquid, add the orange and peppermint essential oils, or extracts. Stir.

6. Pour the chocolate into the brownie pan and spread it out evenly.

7. Cover and refrigerate for 4 hours before serving.

Makes 4 servings. Each serving contains:

Calories: 264   Fat: 12g   Sodium: 45mg

Carbs: 38g   Sugar: 35.5g   Protein: 4g

- Gluten-Free
- Nut-Free
- Vegetarian

Pumpkin Pie Pudding Janie Steele, Moore, OK

Prep. Time: 20 minutes

Cooking Time: 3 hours

Ideal slow-cooker size: 2-qt.

15-oz. can pumpkin 12-oz. can evaporated skim milk ¾ cup granulated Splenda®

½ cup buttermilk baking mix 2 eggs, beaten 2 tsp. pumpkin pie spice 1 tsp. lemon zest whipped topping, optional

1. Combine all ingredients except whipped topping. Mix until smooth.

2. Cover and cook on Low for 3 hours.

3. Serve with whipped topping, if desired.

Makes 4 servings. Without whipped cream, each serving contains:

Calories: 254   Fat: 6g   Sodium: 488mg

Carbs: 23g   Sugar: 7g   Protein: 12.5g

- Nut-Free
- Vegetarian

Vanilla Caramel Dip Hope Comerford, Clinton Township, MI

Prep. Time: 5 minutes

Cooking Time: 45 minutes–1 hour

Ideal slow-cooker size: 1½-qt.

13 unwrapped gluten-free or regular caramels

1 oz. plus 1 tsp. heavy cream 1 tsp. vanilla extract apples, for dipping

1. Spray crock with nonstick spray.

2. Combine caramels, heavy cream, and vanilla in crock.

3. Cover and cook on Low for 45 minutes to 1 hour, or until completely melted.

4. Serve with apple slices for dipping.

Makes 4 servings. Without apple slices, each serving contains:

Calories: 335   Fat: 20g   Sodium: 177mg

Carbs: 55g   Sugar: 47g   Protein: 3.5g

- Gluten-Free
- Nut-Free
- Vegetarian

Spicy Milk Steamer Anita Troyer, Fairview, MI

Prep. Time: 10 minutes

Cooking Time: 1 hour

Ideal slow-cooker size: 3-qt.

4 cups milk

¼ cup brown sugar 1 tsp. cinnamon ½ tsp. nutmeg ½ tsp. cloves

1. Add all ingredients to the crock and stir to mix well.

2. Heat on Low for 1 hour, watching to make sure it doesn't get too hot.

3. Serve in mugs and may garnish with cinnamon sticks.

Makes 4 servings. Using whole milk, each serving contains:

Calories: 191   Fat: 8g   Sodium: 98mg

Carbs: 27g   Sugar: 29g   Protein: 8g

- Gluten-Free
- Soy-Free
- Vegetarian
- Nut-Free

Vanilla Cream Coffee Anita Troyer, Fairview, MI

Prep. Time: 8 minutes

Cooking Time: 2–2½ hours

Ideal slow-cooker size: 3- qt.

1 cup water

3 cups milk

¾ cup heavy cream 3 tsp. instant coffee 3 Tbsp. vanilla syrup

1. Add all ingredients to crock and stir to mix well.

2. Heat on Low for 2–2½ hours.

3. Serve in mugs.

Serving Suggestion: Top mug with whipped topping as a garnish.

Makes 4 servings. Without whipped cream, each serving contains:

Calories: 289   Fat: 24g   Sodium: 92mg

Carbs: 15g   Sugar: 16g   Protein: 6g

- Gluten-Free
- Soy-Free
- Nut-Free
- Vegetarian

Mississippi Iced Tea MarJanita Geigley, Lancaster, PA

Prep. Time: 15 minutes

Cooking Time: 2 hours

Ideal slow-cooker size: 3-qt.

3 black tea bags

4 cups water

½ cup sugar

1. Place water and tea bags in crock.

2. Cook on High for two hours.

3. Pour in glass pitcher and mix in sugar.

4. Refrigerate and serve over ice cubes with a sprig of fresh mint.

Makes 4 servings. Each serving contains:

Calories: 90   Fat: 0g   Sodium: 0mg

Carbs: 64g   Sugar: 64g   Protein: 0g

- Gluten-Free
- Dairy-Free
- Soy-Free
- Nut-Free
- Vegetarian
- Vegan

Winter Juice MarJanita Geigley, Lancaster, PA

Prep. Time: 15 minutes

Cooking Time: 3 hours

Ideal slow-cooker size: 3-qt.

1 qt. water 1 cup fresh cranberries

1   cup apple cider

¼ cup orange juice ¼ cup sugar

¼ cup lemon juice ½ pack mulling spices

1. Combine all ingredients into crock.

2. Mix thoroughly.

3. Cover and cook for 3 hours on Low.

4. Strain the mulling spices out of the juice.

5. Serve warm as a tea or refrigerate and serve as an afternoon spritzer.

Makes 4 servings. Each serving contains:

Calories: 199   Fat: 0g   Sodium: 5mg

Carbs: 29.5g   Sugar: 26.5g   Protein: 0g

- Gluten-Free
- Dairy-Free
- Soy-Free
- Nut-Free
- Vegetarian
- Vegan

THE COMPLETE BEGINNERS GUIDE TO INTERMITTENT FASTING FOR WEIGHT LOSS

SCHEDULED DIETS FOR HEALTHY AND SUSTAINABLE WEIGHT LOSS

INTRODUCTION

The term "intermittent fasting" simply means avoiding certain foods or substances for short periods of time. Both the fasting period and the opportunity to eat are essential components. When fasting, you abstain from all food, whether it contains calories or not. However, some forms of fasting allow you to drink water or tea. After a fast, you have an opportunity period during which you can eat as much as you want as long as you do so in a sensible and healthy manner.

Even if you follow a strict intermittent fasting regimen, you should keep in mind that it is not a magic weight loss cure-all. It's unrealistic to expect to lose 20 pounds in a single week. You can lose a steady amount of weight over a period of time if you stick to a strict diet.

It's important to consult with your doctor before deciding which diet is best for you, as there are many options. It's possible that intermittent fasting will work for you if you're always on the go and have little time to eat healthily. You will do much better if you adopt other healthy eating habits that are more concerned with the types of nutrients that you consume if you are a foodie and always conscious of food in your environment, however.

In your quest for better health, intermittent fasting should be a part of your overall plan.

As a beginner, you may wonder why you need to fast, given the discomfort you will experience. I'll give you a few examples, but there are many more.

-Your metabolic rate is boosted as a result of this process.

- Your body's fat stores are depleted quickly.

-You have the ability to control your desire to eat.

-As a result, your blood pressure is brought back to a more healthy range.

-You're able to keep your blood sugar levels at an ideal level.

- Your heart is operating normally.

As a result, you should be well-versed in the foundations upon which this program is built before beginning. An unwavering commitment to achieving your goal is necessary, as is an unwavering focus on providing the best possible care for your body, as well as making regular exercise an integral part of your daily routine.

You don't have to stock up on a specific type of food if you're doing intermittent fasting. Instead, you should eat slowly and deliberately, keeping in mind that the food you consume has the potential to either benefit or harm your health. Fasting will be much easier for you if you adopt a more holistic approach to your eating habits.

Implement a plan to achieve and maintain the desired outcomes.

So, you've decided to try fasting for the first time. Turn the page to see what's on the upcoming page.

CHAPTER ONE

FASTING

In ancient times, people fasted for a variety of reasons, including improving their health and extending their lives. Aside from the fact that intermittent fasting has been discussed in religious texts and by some of the most renowned philosophers and great thinkers, it's clear that fasting isn't just a new fad.

Anyone who has tried to lose a few pounds has been confronted with the question of when and how much to eat while doing so. In addition to this, fasting provides answers to many other questions. When the solution to losing weight is right in front of you, there's no need to waste time worrying about it. In an attempt to regain their health, many people have engaged in outlandish dietary practices, all to no avail. So, why not take advantage of the powerful healing properties of intermittent fasting? All cultures and faiths have used fasting as a way to achieve a specific goal for thousands of years. Individuals who don't understand what fasting entails are always disgusted when the word is mentioned in conversation. People think it's all about self-deprivation and self-starvation. However, this is a fundamentally flawed approach. Those who are starving are those who are unable to obtain food due to a lack of choice or access.

You can't eat them because they're beyond your reach. As a result, you have no idea when or where your next meal will be. If you're looking for an example, look no further than the ravaged regions of the world or countries that are suffering from extreme drought and starvation. People who are caught up in these situations have no choice but to be deprived of food, which has no beneficial effect on their health. For the most part, fasting is an act that you choose to engage in for a variety of reasons, including health, religion, and more.

The length of a fast is determined by the individual and the reason for the fasting. Have you ever thought about making fasting a regular part of your life? Take, for example, a day in which you eat dinner late at night, then go to bed and don't eat anything for several hours. A "breakfast" is your first meal of the day after you get out of bed. You've just broken a fast you started the night before, and this is a common occurrence.

People's health and spiritual well-being have long been recognized by great thinkers and philosophers throughout history. Fasting was promoted by Hippocrates, Aristotle, and Plato, among others. Rather than using medication, they advocated for fasting as a method of healing. When you're sick, the last thing on your mind is food, haven't you noticed? This is nature's way of acting as a doctor to help the body heal itself. the same as

To quote Hippocrates correctly, "When you are sick and consume food, you are feeding your illness." This is a form of self-preservation that has been ingrained in our DNA since the beginning of time.

Fasting also improves our ability to react, think, and carry out tasks. How do you feel now that you've eaten a substantial meal? Most likely, you'll be sleep-deprived, drowsy, and unable to concentrate on anything for long periods of time. It's because your brain is getting less blood because it's being diverted to your digestive system. For the duration of digestion, which can take several hours, your body goes into a state similar to shock or coma. A few hours that, if experienced frequently, can be harmful to your health. Because fasting always leaves you with a lot of energy and your cognitive faculties intact, it prevents this dangerous phenomenon from occurring.

When you fast for religious or spiritual reasons, your body is cleansed or detoxified. Fasting is an important part of many religions, including Christianity, Islam, and Buddhism. If you're looking for a practice that's both beneficial to your body and your mind, you'll find that yoga is one of the best ways to do so.

Muslims fast from dawn to dusk every day of the month of Ramadan, and the prophet Mohammad advised his followers to do the same.

Weekly at the very least. During the day, Buddhists eat only once and fast until the next morning. As part of their normal eating habits, Buddhists may go through periods of fasting where they consume no food at all. Lent is a 40-day fasting period observed by Christians to commemorate Jesus Christ's crucifixion and resurrection. Every day at sunset is when the individual has their first meal, and they do not eat or drink anything until the following evening. The Orthodox Christians, on the other hand, fast for nearly half the year. Fasting is an important part of many cultures around the world, in addition to major religious institutions.

If you want to reset your body and get rid of toxins, intermittent fasting may not be the best option for you. As a general rule, those with serious health issues should consult their doctor before embarking on any kind of fasting program. There are a lot of diet fads out there, but this new eating habit is not one of them. Instead, keep in mind that this is a strategy for pre-planning your meal times.

It takes a tremendous amount of effort and time to diet because you're constantly battling the urge to eat or not eat. In the process of trying to forget about food, your life force is slowly being drained away. There's nothing wrong with dieting as a means of achieving your fitness goals.

Fasting, on the other hand, is a breeze once you learn the ropes. To lose weight

If you're looking to lose weight, this is an excellent option. With the help of this method, you can develop the mindset that your body does not require constant nourishment. The constant stress of digesting food can be relieved by taking a break. While your digestive system rests, your blood is cleansed and your mind is free to contemplate life's other essentials, such as things other than food. Because your digestive system doesn't have to work as hard to break down food, when you fast, the energy you save can be used to repair your gut wall, reduce the number of antigens your immune system has to contend with, and boost the digestive glands' productivity exponentially. Drinking plenty of fluids during a fast can help flush out toxins from the body.

Is it really a good idea to begin your fast on a Monday, when you already have a ton on your plate? That's not a good idea because it would defeat the purpose of the program entirely. Fasting necessitates a drastic reduction in your daily activities. Reflect on the things in your life that are most important to you. The point is to put your foot on the brake pedal and stop your regular daily activities when you plan to fast so that you can connect with your spirit man. This is important. In the absence of prayer, spend some quiet time in reflection, rest, or doing something meaningful that doesn't put you under too much pressure. Be somber during this time and make it a habit to eliminate any distractions that could jeopardize your goals. conservation of energy

You should prioritize peace and quiet for that particular day.

Once your mind accepts that eating isn't necessary all the time, fasting becomes a lot easier. You say that's impossible, don't you? Quite the contrary, in fact. Developing your strengths and minimizing any potential weaknesses is as simple as learning the material and putting it into practice on a regular basis. In the end, it's up to your willpower and determination to see things through.

CHAPTER TWO
RULES OF YOUR DIET

Your level of activity has an impact on when and what you eat. You should consume more carbohydrates than other nutrients on days when you have to go to work or engage in strenuous activities. Consuming foods high in good fats and protein is essential on days when you're taking it easy, no matter what your level of physical activity may be. No matter what your goals are, it's impossible to overstate the importance of eating whole foods.

Weight loss is defined as a reduction in body weight. It occurs when your daily calorie intake falls short of your ideal intake. You must consume fewer calories than you expend in order to lose weight. If you're trying to shed some pounds, you're going to need to be a little more specific about your goal weight. It's fat that most people envision when they think of obesity. Unfortunately, most of us will experience some loss of muscle mass as a side effect of our efforts to shed extra pounds. What can you do to avoid this? This is where your fat reserves serve as a shield. A large portion of the calories we consume each day are used to break down our muscle mass. In order for this to occur, you must have a calorie deficit in your daily calorie intake. In order to keep track of how many calories you eat, the "energy consumer"

In this case, it is the muscle that must be eliminated.

This is a far cry from the prehistoric times when man had to hunt and move around constantly in search of food and shelter. As their fate depended on it, the muscles were always put to use. Modern men's muscle mass pales in comparison to that of ancient men because so many of us are couch potatoes who can't be bothered to get up and move. As a result, it is critical that we maintain our muscle mass while simultaneously working to reduce adipose tissue through daily physical activity. By gradually reducing your calorie intake, you can prevent your fat deposits from being wiped out and your energy needs from then shifting to your muscle. A gradual adjustment to the new calorie limit will allow your body to get used to the change. As each of us has unique caloric requirements, finding a state of caloric balance can be a challenge. Food nutrients, such as carbohydrates, proteins, and fats, are used to provide the calories needed for a healthy diet. Knowing how many calories you burn on a daily basis depends on a variety of factors, including your gender, age, health, and the activities that you partake in. Calculate your calorific maintenance by keeping track of your daily caloric intake and weight for a few weeks. Your caloric needs would be met at an ideal weight if you were gaining or losing weight by making minor adjustments to your diet.

CALORIE AND FOOD TYPES

Calories are calories, no matter how you slice it. As long as you have it, you'll be able to carry out your daily tasks. This means that there is no such thing as a "right" or "wrong" food in this context; rather, there are foods with excessively high caloric content and foods with inadequate caloric content. To gain 10 pounds of body mass, you can eat 1 pound of food A every day for four weeks; to lose 20 pounds of your body mass, you can do the same thing with food B every day for four weeks. Calorie counts are the only thing separating the various food groups.

Let's take a second look at food now. I told a lie. There are foods that are bad for you, and there are foods that are good for your body. There are so many additives and coloring agents in the so-called "bad foods" that eating them causes major harm to your system. Despite the abundance of these foods on the shelves of supermarkets, it is possible to limit your intake and even avoid them if you so desire. The best way to take care of and safeguard your health is to consume organic food that has undergone minimal processing. It's difficult to avoid processed foods in this day and age, but it is possible. You can begin by gradually eliminating processed foods from your diet and replacing them with whole, organic foods. It may take some time for you to get used to the new diet, but health will benefit greatly from these changes.

HUNGER IS NOT STARVATION

There is a significant distinction between hunger and starvation that should be made clear. You've probably had that overwhelming desire to eat everything in sight because your stomach is rumbling. There is no need to end your fast because of this. The only thing they're feeling is a pang of hunger. So, what are your options here? Distract yourself from it and attend to more important matters. I'm confident that you won't be buried alive if you skip a few meals. Your body was built to survive longer periods of time with no food than you are currently capable of. Because you aren't starving, you aren't going to die. It's a common misconception that fasting causes a decrease in metabolic rate. You cannot go three days without food in an intermittent fasting program because your body's metabolism slows down after 72 hours of fasting. A day's fast is the longest most people can go without food.

Fasting can cause abdominal pain, which is a warning sign that something is wrong. That is not a sign of hunger, and you should contact your doctor right away. As a result of being conditioned to receive food at specific times of the day, your body experiences hunger as a response. Due to your hectic work schedule, it is almost certain that you will miss breakfast if you eat three square meals a day at 8 am, 2 pm, and 7 pm.massive hunger pangs between the hours of 8:30 and 9:15 a.m. Every time it happens, it's like clockwork. When you first begin your intermittent fasting regimen, you will experience hunger pangs, but over time, you will be able to ignore them. In order to get your body used to the new practice, you need to reset your feeding mechanism. As soon as you get the hang of it, you'll only feel the need to eat when you have time to do so. It all comes down to your willpower and mental fortitude to see things through to the end. The power of the mind over the body.

CHAPTER THREE

TYPES OF FASTING

You have complete freedom to experiment with any of the fasting methods I discuss. These diets all follow the same principle: restricting calorie intake in the morning and allowing it in the evening. As it is, it is unfortunate that our eating habits have become so out of whack that we eat all day long without any time to allow our digestive systems to recharge. From 6 a.m. to 6 p.m., one should eat, and from 6 p.m. to 6 a.m., one should fast. With all the late dinners and late-night snacks, it's almost impossible to practice, I hear you say. As a result of the widening of the eating window, your body is now at risk of suffering greatly.

THE WARRIOR DIET

In this fasting strategy, you skip meals during the day and then binge on food later in the evening. For the most part of the day, you don't want to eat anything for breakfast, lunch, or snack. Dinner is the perfect time to satisfy all of your dietary needs. Eating for only four hours during the 20 hours of fasting is known as the 20:4 type of fasting. Fasting using this technique three times a week on average will lead to a total of twenty-four hours of fasting time during the course of a week.

Starting out with intermittent fasting, this method is probably the simplest to follow. You'll love it if you're a fan of big, calorie-packed meals like this. The warrior diet is a simple transition from your normal eating habits because you can begin by eating a small amount of calories during the day before having a large dinner at night. Your caloric intake during the day will gradually decrease, leaving only dinner for you to consume. When you first start out, stick to water and nutritious fruits and vegetables as snacks. Keep a close eye on your caloric intake during this time period to ensure you are getting enough protein and healthy fats. Fasting for at least 18 hours is the most important rule.

In spite of the fact that this type of fasting can be a challenge to begin with, always make an effort to avoid eating any important meals outside of the feeding window. In addition, it's important to keep things consistent. Eat breakfast and lunch every day, even if you've gone on a fast for one day.

Consider that your feeding window, which is about four hours, may not fall on a dinnertime. You can eat it for any meal of the day, not just breakfast. Suppose your feeding window is for breakfast, and after the feeding window for eating in the morning is over, you eat nothing else for the rest of the day until the feeding window for dinner comes around

Next morning. If you choose to eat lunch, the same rules apply.

LEAN GAINS

Many health-conscious people swear by this method of fasting. If you do this, you'll eat your first meal at lunch and your second meal at dinner. There is an 8-hour feeding window and a 16-hour fasting period here. You'll eat dinner at 8 p.m. if you eat lunch at 12. Keep your first meal of the day light and fruit- and vegetable-heavy if you must eat something before that. Fasting for seven days a week results in 112 hours of fasting, which is longer than the typical 12 hours of fasting. If you're a bodybuilder or weightlifter, why not give this method a try? It's never a bad thing to have a little extra muscle mass, and a ripped physique is definitely appealing.

Protein is essential for the body's tissue construction, so it should be consumed in large quantities in the diet. Carbohydrates in your diet should be higher on days when you plan to work out than on non-training days. First meal intake should be higher on days when you don't plan to go to the gym, and lower on days when it isn't necessary to go to the gym. Fasting periods should be scheduled so that they coincide with times when you are sleeping if you are an athlete.

ALTERNATE DAY FAST

You can only feed for a maximum of twelve hours in a forty-eight-hour period using this technique. After eating breakfast at 8 am on Tuesday, you'll be in the feeding window until 8 pm. On Thursday at 8 a.m., the fasting period will come to an end. That only means that you fast all day on Wednesday, and then begin the process again on Thursday. To prepare yourself for the fatty foods to come, you may want to eat whatever you can get your hands on. However, I advise you to keep it healthy.

This is a skill that many people can easily master. Athletes with strict training regimens are not required to practice this because you have a 12-hour feeding window to eat almost anything you want. Consuming calorie-heavy foods should be done cautiously.

ONE DAY FAST

You can fast for 24 hours if you follow this method. It's up to you which day of the week you choose to fast, and you can continue your normal eating habits for the rest of the week. Using this technique, you can consume fewer calories in total.

Weekly. It is possible to lose up to 9% of your weekly caloric intake by going on a full-day fast and then eating only 9000 calories of food for the rest of the week. In order to make up for the meals you missed the day before your fast or to overeat in anticipation of your upcoming fast, there is a tendency to do so. A workaround exists for this. Keep in mind, however, that your caloric intake will still be lower than you are accustomed to because of the calories you are losing so quickly. In the same way as with any fasting method, practice mindfulness and fully engage in your daily activities.

THUMBS UP

Any fasting method you choose should have as its goal the reduction of extra body weight and the attainment of a healthy body weight. It's okay to combine any of the methods in this book with others you've heard of, as long as it doesn't cause you undue discomfort. As difficult as it may be to begin a fasting program, it is recommended that you begin slowly and gradually increase your fasting period. Fasting should be tailored to your daily schedule, so that it doesn't conflict with important events in your life. If you extend your fasting period by more than 12 hours, it will always be beneficial to you. Aiming for the age of 18

At the 16-hour mark, then you're good to go for fasting. As a result of the extra four hours, you've lost some of the calories that you would have consumed. Fasting has a positive impact on your health every single hour.

CHAPTER FOUR

PROS AND CONS

As well as helping you lose weight, it has a number of other advantages. Controlling your hormones, mental and physical processes in your body, and metabolic flexibility are just some of the benefits. If you choose to fast in a way that has a lot of advantages for your body, it can have negative effects on your health. To be clear, the key here is to practice fasting diligently. Consult your doctor before beginning the program if you have any preexisting medical conditions.

MENTAL

Intermittent fasting allows you to see the world in a new light, free from the shackles of food. Your body is accustomed to receiving three meals a day, which you should continue to do. Everything your body asks you to do. Dieting intermittently, on the other hand, is a losing proposition. Assumed it wouldn't work out for some reason? Despite the initial rebellion and infighting, you will adapt to the new change because your body will. To put your health first, there will be no arguing around here. As a result, your attention can now be diverted to more important aspects of your life while your body continues to function properly.

However, intermittent fasting has a downside for those who have had or are currently battling an eating disorder.

Unable to maintain a regular eating schedule. It can lead to an increase in calorie restriction and to a negative focus on the dos and don'ts of fasting being discussed. If you have an eating disorder, you should avoid intermittent fasting.

PHYSIOLOGY

When you fast intermittently, the number of calories you consume each day is reduced. An intermittent fasting program's feeding window makes it nearly impossible to consume the recommended daily caloric intake. A change in your body composition is always a result of this.

Even if you eat a normal amount of calories, this program can help you lose weight. Your body adapts to using fat as a source of energy instead of carbohydrates.

You'll lose muscle mass rather than fat if you restrict your calories rather than fast. The release of cortisol causes an increase in blood sugar levels and an increase in insulin production, which results in a shift from fat to glucose as your primary source of energy.

HORMONES

Hormone sensitivity and control can be greatly enhanced by intermittent fasting. Because fasting lowers insulin levels, the body is more responsive to even small increases in intake. Imagine that you drink six to eight cans of regular coke each day. Most likely, after the second can, you won't feel the effects of the caffeine any more. As a result of drinking a caffeine free coke, your body will become extremely sensitive to even the most minute quantities of caffeine. Due to the link between insulin levels and some debilitating diseases like diabetes, this is of great importance. Resistance to insulin's effects prevents the body from accessing fat stores and impairs its ability to utilize glucose.

If you're a stressed-out person, going on a fast will be counterproductive because your cortisol levels will be skyrocketing. You should study your cycle and know when you are less stressed and fix your fast appropriately because women are very susceptible to monthly hormonal changes.

CHAPTER FIVE

INTERMITTENT FASTING AND YOU

Before embarking on any intermittent fasting regimen, it is imperative that you fully understand your system and whether or not it will work for you. Altering the size or frequency of your meals may be more effective than intermittent fasting for you. There is no such thing as a one-size-fits-all response to a given stimulus. As a result, it is up to you to decide what is best for you.

Do you want to see how it goes for a few days? After that, put a toe in the water to get a feel for it. You can fast for a whole day and not eat a thing. Not a single bite. You'll be in excruciating pain, and you'll be extremely sensitive. At this point, you'll want to give up and walk away from the situation. Within a few hours of skipping a meal, you may notice a decline in your performance, as well as headaches and other symptoms. For those who are capable of making it through this, where do you decide to set up camp? The best way to determine which type of fasting is right for you is to look through the available options. Aside from that, keep in mind that you can continue fasting indefinitely or stop when you reach your ideal weight. Keep a log of your caloric intake, fasting periods, and overall weight loss so you know how much weight you've lost so far.

INTERMITTENT FASTING APPLICATIONS

A fasting program that incorporates features from other fasting programs can always be devised by you. It's important to know what you're doing before attempting this. Here are a few pointers to keep in mind as you work on your program.

Almost every diet has a "fasting" and "eating" period.

When you eat, you're eating for a shorter period of time than when you fast.

Make sure you don't enter starvation mode, which occurs after 38 hours of no food intake, by drinking plenty of water and exercising regularly. Fasting for more than 24 hours at a time is not recommended for health reasons. After that, it's pointless to continue.

IN THE DIRECTION TO EXCELLENCE

The road to a successful fasting regimen can be arduous. Here are a few pointers to get you started.

Get to know the program one step at a time, starting with the basics. Slowly introduce the fasting program into your daily routine. You don't want to jump right into something that may not be designed for your specific needs. Fasting once every three weeks can be a good starting point for those who want to gradually reduce the frequency of their fasts.

It's impossible to use the same program for everyone. So pick a strategy and customize it to your liking.

You'll need to keep a close eye on your body's reaction to an intermittent fasting plan. What you eat, when you eat it, when you exercise, and how many calories you consume are all controlled by your body's internal systems. It is important to take into account all of these factors to ensure that you are in complete control of your fasting program and your weight loss.

If you want to see the fat fall off your bones, don't rush it. Many of us have a short attention span and are willing to abandon diet after diet if they don't produce results right away. If you want to shed pounds in a healthy way, you need to be aware that it is best to do so gradually. It's perfectly acceptable to lose no more than two pounds per week.

Make the most of the time you have while fasting by engaging in your daily routine. You can only guess what will happen if you've been sitting around doing nothing for a long period of time.

Eat when you feel like it, but don't overdo it. In the same way that there is time for everything that we plan, there is time for everything that we plan. So, too, does your eating style. Fasting isn't a one-size-fits-all solution, so find what works for you and stick with it.

RAPID WEIGHT LOSS IN 7 DAYS

A GUIDE TO SUSTAINED HEALTHY WEIGHT LOSS USING JAPANESE DIETS

INTRODUCTION

A weight loss program may seem like a daunting task at first because of the drastic changes you must make in your diet and lifestyle. This is just like any "good" habit, because it's hard compared to the bad habits that we're so accustomed to. There are many ways to get rid of the extra pounds you've been carrying around for far too long. For starters, only alter your diet. Vegetarian diets, which consist primarily of whole grains, vegetables, fruits, and beans, can be surprisingly simple to adopt if you put forth the effort.

Obesity is defined as having more fat in the body than is necessary. Middle-aged people are most likely to suffer from this disorder, but it can also affect those who are younger or older. Those who lead sedentary lifestyles are more likely to be overweight or obese.

As long as fattening foods are readily available and people's eating habits aren't regulated, obesity will be a global problem. Over a billion people on the planet are either overweight or obese, according to studies conducted in 2003.

These numbers were found to have increased by a factor of two in a 2013 study, and this can be linked to technological and societal influences such as increased availability of fast food and sedentary lifestyles.

The body requires the least amount of fat possible in order to function properly and achieve maximum breakthrough. The total amount of fat in the body and the amount of fat consumed have an impact on bodily functions. Having a lot of fat in your body makes your body more vulnerable to disease. The body's ability to absorb shock is jeopardized when it has too little fat to do its job. The immune and thermal insulation systems are both working as they should.

The amount of fat in a person's body also has an impact on reproductive organs and hormonal functions.

People who are obese are more susceptible to illnesses and other health problems. Obesity alters more than just one's physical appearance; it also impairs joint flexibility and one's overall range of motion.

The typical Japanese diets that promote healthy weight loss and overall fitness of the body are described in this book, which will serve to supplement your existing knowledge of healthy weight loss methods. Sumo wrestlers and other athletes who require large amounts of body weight are notable exceptions to the rule for the Japanese.

On the day you begin this program, weigh yourself and keep a daily log of your progress. To keep you motivated, keep a journal in which you can write down your deepest thoughts about why you're on this journey and what you hope to accomplish at its conclusion. So, here are some easy-to-follow instructions on how to get rid of unwanted body weight.

Let's get this show on the road!

CHAPTER ONE

HOW TO DETERMINE EXCESS WEIGHT

The body mass index (BMI) is a useful tool for figuring out how much weight you should be carrying.

Obesity is defined as a BMI of 30 or more.

Pre-obesity is defined as a BMI of 25 to 30.

Overweight or obese is defined as having a BMI of 25 or more.

Weight and other bodily functions can be used to determine a person's fat content, also known as adiposity, in a variety of ways.

DUAL-ENERGY X-RAY ABSORPTIOMETRY (DEXA)

Dexa X-rays were originally designed to measure bone density, but their imaging capabilities allow them to identify fat content in the human body. This technique makes use of the various mass of body fat and tissues, as well as the identification of areas of the body with higher and lower fat concentrations. It is considered one of the most accurate and precise tests for fat because it uses x-ray imaging to show the actual amount of fat. In order to obtain reliable results, DEXA necessitates a large amount of specialized medical equipment and personnel, both of which can be costly.

HYDROSTATIC WEIGHT MEASUREMENTS

Hydrostatic weighing is the second method for determining body fat, and it involves completely submerging the body in water. Submersion in water provides a material that can be used to determine an individual's weight in the water. In order to determine an individual's overall body density, the submerged weight is compared to the dry weight. Estimates of the body fat are made by taking into account the amount of muscle and fat present. In the vast majority of cases, this assessment is nearly perfect. It is also necessary to use trained professionals to administer hydrostatic weighing to get accurate results.

Analysis Of Bioelectrical Impedance

An electric current is passed through the body in order to measure the electrical resistance of the body. Understanding the differences in electrical conductivity between muscle and fat makes calculating one's body fat percentage much simpler. In contrast to the methods described above, this one requires very little training and can be performed at home by non-professionals to estimate their body fat content. Body temperature and hydration can, however, have an impact on the BMI. As a result, this experiment may necessitate some caution.

CALIPERS OR PINCH TEST FOR SKIN FOLDING

Pinching the skin at a specific point on the body and determining the thickness of the resulting field is how this technique works. This type of measurement focuses on the amount of fat that is directly beneath the skin. Because of this analysis, it is possible to determine a person's actual weight without additional testing or measurement. The goal of the test is to find out where the body's excess fat is located on the skin's surface. The amount of body fat available can still be estimated, even if fats that aren't directly deposited under the skin aren't measured.

AN EASY WEIGHTING PROCESS

To find out if your weight is optimal, we'll use a simple weighing scale to get an idea of your current weight and then compare it to the optimal required weight. Despite the fact that this is the least accurate method, it is almost universally used. Body mass, body type and height must all be taken into account in order to accurately measure overweight or obesity. You can start with a scale, but if you have any doubts about the result, you may need to use more sophisticated methods....

SIZE INDEX OF THE BODY

Using 3D software, we can determine the person's true image. It is based on the BVI rating and takes into account the differences in body mass index between individuals. Individual differences in body shape and function are no longer an issue with this technique. The software only needs to know where fats are located, not how much they weigh in total. Because the BVI system takes into account more than just the weight in the abdomen when calculating body mass index, this is an advantage.

CHAPTER TWO

HEALTH IMPLICATIONS OF OBESITY

Obesity and overweight can significantly raise a person's risk of illness and level of health. Some of these health issues can affect both the mother and the baby in the long run, such as obesity-related cancers, heart disease, and diabetes.

PROBLEMS WITH PREGNANCY

Having a C-section may result in a delay in healing, which can have a negative impact on the mother and baby's health. Obesity during pregnancy raises blood pressure, which is bad for both the mother and the baby in the long term. It's important for pregnant women with preeclampsia to be treated and monitored in order to avoid these dangers. Gestational diabetes, or high blood sugar during pregnancy, can be caused by carrying around too much fat. As a result of being overweight during pregnancy, these can also occur.

TUBIC RHINITIS

The kidney's primary job is to remove waste and water from the bloodstream. A healthy and active body can be maintained by controlling blood pressure with this supplement. Kidney disease is a condition in which the filtering abilities of the kidneys have been compromised. Waste can accumulate in the body if the filter is not working properly. Overweight and obesity are major risk factors for kidney disease, as are high blood pressure and diabetes. New research shows that obesity can directly cause kidney disease, even if there is no preexisting risk.

FAT LIVING CANCER

Fatty liver disease, also known as non-alcoholic steatohepatitis (NASH), is caused by an overgrowth of fat in the liver. In addition to liver failure and cirrhosis (a scarring of the liver tissue), severe liver damage can be caused by these fatty livers. Unlike alcoholic liver disease, which develops over time as a result of drinking too much alcohol, fatty liver disease does not begin with an excessive intake of alcohol.

OSTEOARTHRITIS

Osteoarthritis is a degenerative disease of the joints that results in swelling, tenderness, and stiffness. Age and injury are frequently linked to this health problem. The lower back, hips, knees, and hands are the most commonly affected areas. Osteoarthritis can be caused by obesity, which is one of the most common risk factors. Inheritance, advancing age, and trauma are all contributing factors.

There is extra strain on joints due to weight gain. The fibrous tissues covering the bones and joints are worn away by the weight of the body and the pressure of fat. Inflammation can be exacerbated by elevated levels of potentially harmful substances in the blood, which may be a consequence of an overweight or obese state.

ANXIETY WHILE SLEEPING

This sleep disorder is characterized by one or more breath pauses. People with this condition may experience heart failure, which is characterized by difficulty and daytime sleepiness. Obesity has been linked to an increased risk of sleep apnea, according to research. This is due to the fact that a person with a larger neck may have a narrower airway than another. Snoring is a common symptom of snoring, which is when someone has trouble breathing because their airways are too small. Breathing may stop for a brief period of time in chronic cases. As a result, sleep apnea may become more common as a result of neck fat accumulation.

STROKE

When your brain's blood supply is cut off, this problem occurs. Ischemic stroke occurs when blood clots form in the artery, preventing blood flow to the brain. Unlike ischemic stroke, hemorrhagic stroke occurs when the blood vessels burst, which is another type of stroke. The risk of a stroke increases when a person's blood pressure is elevated as a result of being obese. Heart disease, hyperglycemia, and high cholesterol are all associated with strokes.

DISEASES OF THE HEART

In this case, a hardening and narrowing of the blood vessel that brings blood to the heart causes this problem. It can cause a wide range of heart-related issues. Increased risk can be expected when the heart does not receive adequate blood supply. The heart may not be pumping enough blood to the body due to a variety of reasons. A heart disease patient may have an abnormal heart rhythm, chest pains, cardiac death, cardiac failure, or a heart attack, among other complications. Health problems that may lead to heart disease are associated with obesity. There are a number of associated health issues, such as diabetes, high cholesterol, and hypertension. The heart has to work harder to pump blood around the body because of excess fat.

EXCESSIVE HYPERTENSION OF THE BLOOD COOLER

This is the amount of force your blood exerts on the artery walls as it flows through them. Every time the heart beats, blood is pumped out of the heart and into the arteries. While there are no symptoms of high blood pressure, it can lead to serious illnesses like kidney failure, stroke, and heart disease. Normal blood pressure is 120/80 mm Hg. Hypertension is defined as a blood pressure reading of 140/90 or higher. Diastolic blood pressure is the lower number and systolic blood pressure is the higher number. Having a larger frame naturally means that the heart has to work harder, which in turn increases blood pressure.

DIABETIC TYPE 2 (T2)

Blood sugar levels are elevated in people with type 2 diabetes. Obesity and overweight are both linked to type 2 diabetes at different levels. Diabetes is the 7th leading cause of death in the United States, according to a study conducted in 2009. The most common causes of diabetes are obesity, a poor diet, and a lack of physical activity. Approximately 80% of those who have type 2 diabetes are also obese. Even though the direct link between obesity and diabetes isn't clear, studies have shown that overweight people's cells change, making them more resistant to insulin. This means that insulin resistance reduces the ability of cells to absorb glucose, resulting in elevated blood sugar levels. Type 2 diabetes risk may be reduced through weight loss, which can be achieved through exercise or a reduction in sugar intake.

CHAPTER THREE

METHODS OF WEIGHT LOSS THAT WON'T WORK

Despite the fact that there are numerous workout and diet regimens promising maximum weight loss with minimal effort, one thing is for certain: some of these tips don't work, and even if they do, the side effects may be detrimental to your health. As a result, you should consult your doctor before embarking on any weight-loss regimen. When your weight is linked to a medical condition, you need to be extremely cautious about the diet you choose. If you don't want to waste your time and money on weight loss methods that won't be effective for you in the long run, consider these strategies that are more likely to yield long-term results.

GOING FAT AND SUGAR-FREE

There is no need to completely avoid the consumption of fat despite the negative effects it has on the body. Fat is, in fact, one of the essential nutrients our bodies need to stay healthy. On the other hand, you may be avoiding sugar while increasing your intake of fat, or vice versa. Sugar-free products, on the other hand, may contain artificial sweeteners that contribute to weight gain as well. Even sugar-free drinks contain flavor enhancers, which can lead to an increase in sugar consumption. No matter how hard you try, the synthetic fat- or sugar-free products fail. As a result, you're more likely to overindulge on chemicals than healthy fats and sugars. Instead, consume only natural, organic foods in an effort to shed pounds and improve your overall health and wellness.

LOADING UP ON PROTEIN

We've all fallen into the trap of believing that increasing our protein intake will lower our caloric intake and, as a result, our body fat. By restricting your diet to protein alone, you are depriving your body of important nutrients like fat and carbohydrate that it needs. No matter how much weight you want to lose, you must eat a healthy, well-balanced diet in order to stay fit and maintain a healthy weight. Overconsumption of any one nutrient is harmful to your health. One food group is not enough. Gaining the strength to do the fat-burning exercises you need is a delicate balancing act.

COUNTING CALORIES

Do you believe that fat storage increases in direct proportion to caloric intake? If this is the case, you've got your head in the wrong place. Optimal nutrition does not necessitate a strict calorie-counting regimen. Even though it may come as a shock to you, not all calories are created equal, and what goes into your body affects what comes out of it. Your body's function will also be affected by the timing of calorie intake. Calories from various fruits and foods have varying effects on your body because they cause a variety of reactions. Empty calories and quality calories are two distinct concepts. When it comes to consuming high-quality calories, sticking to whole, unprocessed foods is your best bet.

STAYING AWAY FROM SNACKS

It is not necessary to completely give up on snacks in order to avoid them. Snacking in moderation is key to maintaining a healthy weight and staying away from unhealthy diets, but moderation is only possible if you adhere to a strict snacking schedule. No matter how bad your cravings are, allowing yourself a few treats now will help you make better food choices in the future. You don't have to go to great lengths to avoid eating in order to lose weight if you stick to healthy, nutritious meals.

LOW-CALORIE DIETS

Foods with fewer or controlled calories have long been part of weight loss plans and diets. Even if you follow a strict diet plan, it will be useless if you can't get your body to adjust to it without relapsing or turning to unhealthy foods. Diets like these deprive your body of nutrients and slow down your metabolic rate. Taking reasonable-calorie diets on a regular basis will solve the problem. Only eat what your body and health require, and you'll be doing yourself a favor.

GETTING RID OF DAIRY

Why do most dieters avoid all dairy products, including ice cream, cheese, and milk? Milk is an essential part of the human diet, and the body requires a large amount of it. When the body has enough calcium, it burns fat at a much faster rate than when it doesn't. You can gain weight while trying to lose weight if you don't get enough calcium in your diet. Even if it's low-fat, make sure to include dairy in your shopping list.

DETOXING

In order to rid the body of toxins, detox is an extreme measure that is taken. The goal of detox products is to keep the colon clean, but experts say that this is a complete waste of time. Your kidneys and liver will take care of the rest. Juices used in these detox diets may contain sugar and therefore not be suitable for people of all weights.

SKIPPING BREAKFAST IS NOT AN OPTION

For the well-informed, a nutritious breakfast is an essential part of one's daily routine. If you want to lose weight, you can't keep skipping breakfast. It's better to eat something light in the morning than to skip breakfast altogether. For this reason, skipping breakfast can lead to overeating later on, which can lead to binge eating, which can lead to an increase in your fat level. The effects of skipping breakfast include larger lunch portions and a desire to eat again before dinner.

CRASH DIET

Crash diets do more harm than good to the body. In order to be able to wear that dress by the end of the week, you must be able to do so now. The body does not benefit from a diet high in fruits and vegetables. Choosing a diet plan is a very important decision. No matter what changes you make, you must choose a diet that includes all of the necessary nutrients and food groups, as well as a specific calorie count. Your ultimate goal should be to have a healthy body. When you return to a normal diet after a period of fasting or calorie restriction, your body will have a difficult time burning calories.

FOOD OUTSIDE THE HOME

Consuming high-calorie foods on one day a week may not be beneficial to your health. Restaurant food is higher in calories than food prepared at home, and you won't know how much you've eaten until you've finished. When it comes to weight loss, women who eat home-cooked meals are more likely to shed the pounds than those who dine out once a week. You can eat out at least once a month and still lose weight and achieve your health goals if you limit your dining out to once a month.

CHAPTER FOUR

JAPANESE RECIPES AND STEPS TO MAINTAIN GOOD HEALTH THE JAPANESE WAY

THE 7 DAYS JAPANESE WEIGHT LOSS PLAN

This program consists of diet plans that will help you lose weight fast. You are advised to best drink water in between meals to meet the requirement of the requirement for 8 cups of water daily plan.

Note that bread, alcohol, sugar, salt and other unhealthy menus are not acceptable during the dieting period. You are advised not to make changes or relapse for the seven days' duration to enjoy the fullness of the Japanese menu. According to a study, once you double the time of dieting over, you will lose up to 15 pounds all depending on the eight-day before you started. Also, avoiding relapse is essential to reach the level of weight loss. As a caution, you should not repeat this diet plan more than twice a year to prevent metabolism imbalance in the body. You should put in mind that the diet is low calorie and you may need to stop in case of drastic changes in your body.

DAY 1

Breakfast: black or green tea.

Lunch: steak, 8 oz. and any fruits.

Dinner: olive oil, romaine lettuce salad, 8 oz. of broiled steak, and two hard-boiled eggs.

DAY 2

Breakfast: black coffee

Lunch: olive with lettuce salad, romaine in particular. 15 oz. broiled or steamed chicken breast.

Dinner: olive sucked with romaine salad lettuce, sliced fresh carrot, three hard-boiled eggs. Lemon juice should be included.

DAY 3

Breakfast: two carrots, dressed with lemon juice. Fresh carrots are preferable where available.

Lunch: unsalted tomato, 2 cups. 17 oz. Large boiled, steamed or broiled fish.

Dinner: olive oil with romaine salad, 7 oz. of steak. Three hard- boiled eggs.

DAY 4

Breakfast: green tea

Lunch: fry one large root of fennel or parsnip and consume with apples.

Dinner: 6 oz. steak. Olive oil, with romaine lettuce salad. Three hard-boiled eggs.

DAY 5

Breakfast: black coffee

Lunch: Dress boiled carrots with lemon juice. Olive oil should be included in the boiling process.

Dinner: 3 large fresh carrots and one hardboiled egg.

DAY 6

Breakfast: Black coffee, one toast

Lunch: romaine lettuce salad with olive oil. Boiled, steamed or broiled fish.

Dinner: one low-fat plain yoghurt. 7 oz. Grilled steak.

DAY 7

Breakfast: black coffee or tea

Lunch: add a fresh tomato to an olive oil romaine lettuce. Boiled, steamed or broiled fish.

Dinner: black coffee or tea.

CHAPTER FIVE

LOWER BODY WEIGHT AND GENERAL WELL-BEING

Considering the importance of having optimum body weight, there are diet facts you need to be aware of for losing weight without the need for rigorous exercise and other unhealthy ways or weight loss approach.

DON'T GET THIRSTY

Getting dehydrated is not a good choice and taking lower fat should complement water when necessary. Also, you should resort to non-alcoholic drinks, and resort to natural fruits and fruit juices when needed. 6 to 8 glasses of water are required to aid digestion for optimum fluid flow. This is more important when the weather is hot; you might take four glasses when the weather is cold and achieve optimum digestion.

GET ACTIVE

Regardless of the effort to keep rigorous exercises at bay, being active is very important for achieving proper health. A balanced diet is not enough for achieving the best health and weight. To avoid the risk of developing stroke, heart disease, cancer or type-2 diabetes, it is crucial that you perform simple exercises to keep your body moving. Toxins and wastes are easily ridden, and you will achieve optimum health in the end.

EAT LESS SALT

Your sugar and salt intake should be balanced. To reduce the risk of hypertension, you are required to consume a particular amount of salt on a daily basis. Use the information on food labels to determine the amount of salt in a given food item. A food item having 1.5 per 100g indicates it has a high salt content. For good health, you should not take more than 6g of salt daily. Also, the salt level in the body can be regulated through simple exercises like taking a walk or jogging every morning or evening.

WATCH THAT SUGAR!

Even though sugar has high energy, excess consumption contributes to weight gain in the lower body and the body in general. Sugar can also cause tooth decay among other ailments. You should take note of the things you consume that contain more sugar than your body can handle. Favour unsweetened fruit juices, syrups, and natural honey to reduce your sugar intake. Do not take a bottle of soda if not necessary. Always take more water and eat enough food to lessen the need for soft drinks, which contain the highest amount of sugars we take in every day. Pastries, biscuits, cakes, processed cereals, alcoholic beverages and sugary fizzy drinks should be avoided as much as possible.

WALK AWAY FROM SATURATED FATS

Saturated fats can increase the amount of cholesterol in the blood and therefore enhances the risk of the developing heart disease. On the average, you are not to have more than 30g of saturated fat on a daily basis. Women, in particular, should have just 20g of saturated fat and no more. Watch foods such as pies, lard, butter, cream, s, biscuits, cakes, and hard cheese. These foods contain a significant amount of saturated fats that should be avoided as much as possible. Foods containing unsaturated fats include avocados, oily fish, and vegetable oils.

LOVE THAT FISH

Fish contains vitamins and minerals, and it is an excellent source of protein. The Asians consume fish every day hence their healthy way of life. Fish contains omega-3 fatty acid which helps in preventing heart disease. This oily fish includes pilchards, sardines, fresh tuna, herring, trout, mackerel, and salmon. The non-oily fish include hake, Skake, canned tuna, cod, Coley, and haddock. Choosing a wide variety of fish is always important to explore the extent of the health benefits of consuming fish.

NOTES

THE END

CPSIA information can be obtained
at www.ICGtesting.com
Printed in the USA
BVHW031702170822
644856BV00013B/619